AF255699

Surviving the
Talent Exodus

Navigate the Perfect Storm for Generational Change in the Workplace

By

John Grubbs

Surviving the
Talent Exodus

Navigate the Perfect Storm for Generational Change in the Workplace

By

John Grubbs

Parcam Press

For Amie, Cameron, and Parker
You inspire me daily!

TABLE OF CONTENTS

INTRODUCTION

I recently accompanied my mother on a routine medical appointment. Her physician of over 20 years finally threw in the towel and retired.

While completing the enormous mounds of paperwork required for a new medical provider in today's contradictory electronic world, I noticed a young mother walk into the waiting area with two small children. The mother was in her early twenties, and the children looked to be three and four.

The mother was flanked on both sides by these extremely well kept, and well behaved, young children. The boy was on her right hand, closest to me. While he never made eye contact with me, I noticed something very odd about this young boy. He was carrying a disposable, plastic shopping bag that was inflated to maximum capacity. It was not just the bag that made this a remarkable sight. The boy carried this opaque plastic bag as if it contained his most prized possession. He held the bag firmly and deliberately by both handles while the swollen, air-filled container followed him like a tiny puppy, occasionally kissing the ground gently.

As I pondered the logic of this empty bag, and resisted the temptation to ask, many thoughts entered my mind. After all, we need something to occupy the dullness of the waiting room. Was this bag something he found in the parking lot? Was he in search of trash receptacle to make a deposit?

While there are many possibilities, the optimist in me deduced that this empty grocery sack was his bag of opportunity. I concluded that today will be filled with many opportunities in the mind of that young boy. While following Mom on her errands, he will inevitably encounter many extremely valuable objects to place in this bag. I believe he saw the rest of the day as filled with many opportunities to fill his precious bag and he is going to be ready.

The more I reflect on this young boy, and his attitude, the more I respect his wisdom and untarnished optimism about life. Since his precious lesson, I have made more effort to seek the opportunity of each remarkable day, while being ready to accept the many gifts we receive. Whether it is breakfast with my family, or a pleasant drive to work through the piney trees, I am trying to fill my daily bag with as much as I can each day.

I also notice that we can carry multiple bags depending on the opportunities that we seek, and often find, if we are simply looking. We can find amazing things to go in the bags if we just open our eyes and look around. A cup of coffee with our parents, or a quiet breeze on the patio, can certainly fit into a bag. A successful encounter with a customer, or a new opportunity for my business, also occupy one of my bags. Reading a new book, or acknowledging a friend's Facebook post with a kind comment, can fit into yet another bag.

That little boy taught me that I need to begin every day with an empty bag, and deliberately squeeze as much out of life as is humanly possible. This simple blessing from a small child is a gift I carry in my own daily bag.

This book is something I hope you place in your bag. The lessons will be valuable for you and your organization, especially if you are searching for direction amidst the storm of significant workplace changes.

Think of this writing as a road map into an uncharted location. Old road maps will get you lost because they only describe the way things were, not what they will be in the coming years. While some conclusions are based on speculation, there is a lot of data to support the possibilities suggested here. Keep your mind, and your bag, open as you examine what the workforce will look like in the coming years.

The enormity and the significance of the changes we are about to experience are very real. In many cases of organizational change, the subtle nature of, and the rate of, change cause resistance and even apathy in organizational leaders. They are too focused on the present to see the future. Like the frog that remains in the pot of water until boiled, the gradual change in the workplace may catch us unprepared, or in some cases unwilling, to jump from the boiling pot.

My hope is that each reader finds true value, as well as enjoyment, in the pages of this book. Whether every prediction in this work becomes a reality or not, the exploration that grew into these pages was exciting, humbling, and at times scary.

The generational change is upon us, and to-morrow will find us more deficient in talent from one perspective, while providing us with amazing opportunity from another. Only the wisest leaders will have a perspective that offers both viewpoints. They alone will be prepared for the coming Perfect Storm.

Introduction

"Life does not consist mainly, or even largely,
of facts and happenings. It consists mainly of
the storm of thought that is forever flowing
through one's head."
~Mark Twain

CHAPTER 1
The Perfect Storm

January 1st, 2008 came and went as any typical new year's day. People celebrated the New Year in an array of traditions around the world. The hope of a brand new year brought promise of great things to come. Organizational leaders, captains of industry, managers and entrepreneurs all joined the celebration. There were no headlines of concern, no alarms in the corporate conference room, and no big fuss about the pending storm of change that would besiege most organizations for years to come.

People simply did not notice or even acknowledge the magnitude of change that would reign over most organizations in the United States.

Today, we are facing another date that will far surpass the significance of January 1st, 2008, and again most organizations are unaware and certainly not ready for the pending challenge. According to some estimates, the workplace began losing tens of thousands of Baby Boomers to retirement in 2008.

Imagine a large tub filled with water that represents upwards of ninety million Baby Boomers in the workplace. The birth of 2008 opened the drain, and a huge vortex of this generation began to escape the tub. This evacuation of talent and knowledge will intensify greatly as this population begins to turn sixty-five years old.

Most Boomers want to get the most from social security. They are concerned that the system they have paid into for so many years is on a path that cannot be sustained. Threats of cuts and changes in eligibility are very much on the minds of these workers. The self-induced pressure to leave the workplace will only intensify as millions of Boomer's desire to get out while the getting's good.

Unfortunately, too many organizations will not be prepared to deal with the talent exodus that is upon them.

Not surprisingly, the Boomers are in a wonderful position to leverage their talent. Many retired Boomers are returning to the workplace as consultants, charging as much as three times their previous wage for their services. Retirement is wonderful these days if you have key organizational knowledge that companies cannot do without.

Even more amazing is the fact that some very myopic organizations are actually accelerating the impact by offering early retirement "buyouts" to those with the knowledge, experience, and skills they need to survive in the coming years.

Overlay the exodus of Boomers with the emergence of Generation Y (less than 30 years old) and the very limited supply of Generation X in the middle—and Perfect Storm is upon us.

Meteorologicaly, a Perfect Storm is three storms forming one super storm. As an analogy, it aptly describes what is and will be happening in the workplace. Frightening, most organizations are simply not ready to weather the pending challenges.

The current recession, and the lower demand for talent, have kept the enormity of the problem off the agendas of most executive board rooms. Executives are either ignorant to the demands of the future workplace (when the jobs return) or they are "rolling the dice" by hoping the storm subsides or misses their business.

Regardless of the reason, most companies large and small have no plan and certainly do not have a formal talent strategy. They are conducting business as usual and hoping for the best.

The change facing the workplace is so significant, and yet the preparation is so limited.

Example:

Larry, a veteran manager in an established company, worked his way up the organizational ladder. He is very proud of what he knows and what the company has become over the years. Core metrics like safety and quality have improved greatly under his watchful guidance. The company is relatively profitable, and he shares in that profit. He is five years from retirement and is not sure what he is going to do with his time when he retires.

Thomas is the youngest manager on the corporate payroll. He is frustrated by the seemingly uninterested group of leaders at the top of the organization. He has a Master's degree, and reads extensively about organizational change and improvement. Every time he offers a suggestion, or constructive criticism about the company, he his rebuffed or ignored. He has many ideas about how to make the company more effective; however, he feels no one cares.

Thomas is beginning to think this job is not where he needs to be. He likes the industry, and enjoys his work. He feels that he is adequately compensated, but he cannot figure out why a company would pay him so much and not listen to a word he has to say. He is going to update his resume soon and see what else is out there for him.

Mary is a manager who recently accepted a position with the company. She has twenty years experience in her field, and feels like she just landed the perfect job with an established company that has a good reputation. She cannot figure out why turnover is so high at such a great organization. She is excited about moving her family for this new job. She thinks she may even move up if the opportunity presents itself.

These three employees all work for the same company, and they are on a collision course.

Larry is comfortable with the current state of the company, and does not see any reason to rock the boat. "If it is not broken, do not fix it," is his mantra. When ideas for organizational change are offered, he thinks about the many times the company started something new only for it to fade. He has become so battle-scarred that he resists any change. Though not intentional, he has become a large hurdle for improvement in the company.

Thomas has offered more ideas to improve than he can remember. Although polite and professional, no one seems to give him much credibility. He is making almost $100,000 a year and is willing to walk away during this terrible recession to find another job. Life is too short to waste a moment in an organization that does not utilize his skill set. He is willing to stay, but at this point he thinks it is best to look elsewhere for employment.

Mary is still in the "honeymoon" period with her new job. She is so busy that she has not noticed the organizational challenges around her. She is focused on learning the ropes of her department and does not participate in the politics.

The Perfect Storm is brewing.

Mary may very well be the only manager (of the three) left in the company 12 months from now.

The company is offering early retirement as a method for cutting payroll expenses. Larry will soon be made aware of the retirement package. Though not planning to leave, the incentives are very good for him and his family, and, when offered, he will accept the package.

Thomas has already notified his LinkedIn network that he is looking for another job. His seven years with the company since college, along with his MBA, will certainly land him another job. He will be gone shortly after Larry.

Mary will be left doing three jobs within six months. She is starting to realize that her hourly rate (if you calculate it since she is salaried) is far less than some of the veteran front-line employees because she now works 65 hours a week. She is under tremendous stress at home and at work. She feels like she can work it out and can get things under control, but she doesn't yet see a light at the end of the tunnel.

Welcome to the Perfect Storm!

The Perfect Storm

13

**"Money won't create success,
the freedom to make it will."**
~Nelson Mandela

CHAPTER 2
Retain the Best

How do you retain your best employees? Employee retention is becoming the largest challenge to business success. Companies are competing for the same pool of qualified applicants. They are also attempting to entice the best from their competition without shame.

The problem is that these desirable employees know their value, and are not ashamed to leave their current employer for a better offer. Even during tough times, skilled employees are perched in the driver seat, and starving companies will do almost anything to get them.

Can you attract, and keep, good employees without throwing money at the problem? Throughout this book, I will discuss the five things you can do to improve employee retention as the shift in generations:

1. **Trash the traditional schedule:** Flexibility and time off are critical for long-term retention. Four 10-hour shifts per week will attract more interest than five 8-hour shifts.

2. **Use technology:** A clean, bright work environment, with modern technology to make work less physically demanding, will keep employees, even when someone offers more money.

3. **Train, train, and train:** The more learning opportunities you provide, the stronger your bonds with your team will be. Training provides information, and you cannot share too much with your people.

4. **Forget control:** Control is just an illusion. Empower your people to solve problems and meet challenges. If your team feels challenged, they are more likely to stay, even when they are offered more money elsewhere.

5. **Communicate:** Remember, your people need information. Why are you doing what you are doing? How is it beneficial to the individual, organization, and the public? The more information you share, the better

employees will feel about being on your team.

Businesses that fail to apply these five areas into their work environment will be at risk as the younger generation rises to prominence in business.

Example:

A business operates on an ongoing basis with expectations that workers commit fifty to sixty hours of work per week. The pay and benefits are wonderful. Unskilled young workers from a near-by large city are in endless supply. These young workers make great money with the overtime they receive. The turnover rate for the factory is roughly 70 percent.

The jobs require extensive up-front training to understand the process and equipment. The company provides this training and commits significant resources to ensure the training is effective. In fact, with only 250 employees, the company spends approximately $800,000 per year on turnover. This figure includes recruiting, training, and other hiring expenses.

Yet, the management team is unwilling to see that the problem is not the workforce; it is the expectations for work that do not coincide with the values of the generation they seek to employ. In other words, the problem exists with the company that is not willing to bend or adapt to the community they seek to hire.

"Do not confine your children to your own learning, for they were born in another time."
~Chinese Proverb

CHAPTER 3
Understanding the Generations

There are three generations represented in the workforce today: the Baby Boomers, Generation X, and Generation Y. Each generation has it's own characteristics, attitudes toward work, and relationship with the organizations they work for.

As leaders, it is important that we understand the characteristics of each of the generations on our team because then we'll be better equipped to lead. We will also better understand people at work, and be less frustrated when their values and work ethic are different from our own.

If we don't learn about the generations, and expect others to conform to our perspective of work, we will be ineffective in leadership. Worse, our team will begin to have frustrations and problems. Wouldn't it be better to be informed, and to lead the different generations appropriately?

Baby Boomers

Baby Boomers are the oldest people in the workplace. While they are retiring in great numbers, they still have a tremendous influence on the workplace. The represent a bridge to the way things used to be.

Baby Boomers represent Americans born after World War II, between 1946 and 1963. After World War II, America was one of the few developed nations not destroyed by war. The Baby Boomers experienced a period of high prosperity unlike any other in the history of America. The wartime factories were converted to peacetime manufacturing entities, and anyone looking for work could find a good job that allowed a comfortable middle class existence.

I often call this period the "Leave it to Beaver Era" that allowed Dad to work in a good job, and Mom to stay at home to raise the family. Americans were able to flourish and prosper, while the rest of the developed world struggled to recover and rebuild. Europe and Japan bought everything we could make, and business experienced a period of growth. This period of affluence and privilege influenced how Baby Boomers saw this country and life.

In the workplace, Baby Boomers are hard working and loyal. They focus on work and professional accomplishment; thus, they tend to be motivated by status and positions of prestige. They can be dedicated, passionate, and resourceful when it comes to work.

Baby boomers consider themselves to be a special generation. They create a unique lifestyle by being the first people who defined the world in terms of generations. They built the business world that we know, and now they are leaving it in great numbers through retirement.

Generation X

The generation that I belong to, Generation X, represents about 40 million Americans born between 1964 and 1980. We make up the period of birth decline after the baby boom, and we are significantly smaller than previous and succeeding generations. We are almost insignificant when it comes to the workplace due to our small numbers, and our influence on the workplace is minimal at best. That is not to say that we do not have a prominent place in the world of work.

We are mostly in our 30's and early 40's today, and our generation tends to be more ethnically diverse and better educated than the Baby Boomers. According to the research, more than 60% of Generation X attended college. We are the middle managers and junior executives of today's business world. We run small businesses and are the professionals that make your life what it is today. We are the dentists, doctors, lawyers and plumbers that hold our society together. We are the counselors, consultants and church leaders that give advice about the very life we live.

Generation X is important because we are responsible for the very existence of Generation Y as parents, teachers and mentors. To say the least, we are influential by virtue of the generation we have created and raised.

In general, Generation X is individualistic. We grew up during an era of two-income families, increasing divorce rates, and a declining economy. In this environment, with our mothers at work, we became latch-key children. At a young age, we became independent, resourceful, and self-sufficient.

In the workplace, Generation X perpetuates these qualities. We value freedom and responsibility. Many in this generation display a casual disdain for authority and structured work hours. We dislike being micro-managed and embrace a hands-off management philosophy.

As we entered the workforce, America shifted from a manufacturing economy to a service economy. This shift, along with the tough economic times in the 1980s, resulted in many of our parents losing hard-earned jobs. Thus, Generation X is less committed to one employer, and are more willing to change jobs to get ahead than previous generations. We adapt well to change, and are tolerant of alternative lifestyles. Generation X is ambitious and eager to learn new skills, but we want to accomplish things on our own terms.

Unlike previous generations, members of Generation X work to live, rather than live to work. They appreciate fun in the workplace, and espouse a work hard/play hard mentality. Generation X managers often incorporate humor and games into work activities.

Generation Y

Generation Y was born during the age of personal computers. For most of their lives, they have had information at their fingertip. As a result, they want to know why. "Because I said so," will not work with them.

Generation Y is the second largest population demographic (sixty to seventy million strong) in society today. Regardless of what you think of them, Generation Y is your future workforce.

If you want good employees who are dedicated to the expansion of your business, you need to provide a workplace that is attractive to Generation Y. This requires you to shed old practices and embrace new ones.

So what management traits will drive away Generation Y?

- Managers who are close-minded, and do not listen to other perspectives and ideas.

- Managers who do not assign meaningful work that creates value for someone or something.

- Managers who do not know what they are doing. Generation Y wants to work for leaders who are also learners.

- Managers who do not know how to train and communicate ideas to others, and who hoard or protect knowledge.

- Managers who do not give respect to younger team members, and who expect respect in return.

- Managers who try to intimidate younger workers through fear.

- Managers who focus on appearance through their own filters and are closed to others' views.

- Managers who resist change and remain focused on the past.

The most significant challenge for Generation Y is the Baby Boomer generation.

Think about the amazing time of change we are living in today. Beginning January 1, 2008, we started losing thousands and thousands of Baby Boomers each day to retirement at age sixty-two. There are not enough Generation X employees to replace the large volume of Baby Boomers leaving the workplace. Generation X is insignificant by virtue of their limited size. Who is left?

That is correct—the future of all successful organizations is dependent on Generation Y. Many studies stress the impact Generation Y will have on the modern business landscape. And, many business leaders are concerned because of the diverging values common to these very different groups.

Generation Y values time off with friends and social events to the point that they will typically not sacrifice their personal life for a career or job. They believe you "can" have it all and do not favor companies that place work or jobs over life. Generation Y believes technology solutions are much more effective than physical labor solutions. They will not tolerate the yelling and screaming of the past, and will leave companies that utilize fear and threats as a management methodology. Generation Y favors flexible schedules based on productive output, rather than the preoccupation with the 40-hour week and typical work schedules of the past.

Moving forward, there are only going be two types of companies. There will be companies that prepare and adjust to attract the best of Generation Y, and there will be companies that fail because they ignore the reality of change associated with this new and dominant generation.

Example:

The pending talent exodus is literally off the radar for Dan's company. He is the chief executive for a small company with a 60-year history. The niche markets and the specialty products they produce have created a comfortable living for 400 employees and their families.

Veteran employees have tremendous knowledge and experience in the work they perform. The 30-year employees have been the backbone of the company for some time. And truthfully, Dan takes the knowledge and experience for granted. No one on the team is thinking about the tremendous loss the team will experience over the next five to ten years.

The younger managers are aggressively working to meet organizational goals that are focussed more on trailing indicators than leading indicators. Dan's company has not significantly changed the metrics by which they run the company in many years.

Mid-level managers in their late 30s and early 40s struggle to find new talent. Young employees are hard to attract because the work environment is hot and the labor can get difficult. While the compensation is quite good, few talented Generation Y applicants exist. Worse, the entry level positions have difficulty retaining hard working employees. Without admitting it, the company is targeting immigrant workers with a perceived strong work ethic.

Veteran employees are retiring in higher numbers. The parties and gold-watch ceremonies happen almost weekly. The cost of the watches concerns human resources; they are looking for more affordable, comparable alternatives to the timepieces.

The remaining veterans form two distinct groups: those preparing for retirement, and those frustrated by the perception of work from the younger employees.

Those preparing for retirement are almost completely disengaged from the work or the future. These smart, capable, and loyal employees coast toward a retirement date. They offer little toward the improvement of the organization. No one asked their opinions about where the organization is headed, nor does it appear that anyone cares what they have to say. Dan has no idea of their feelings or opinions about his company.

The veterans not preparing for retirement are frustrated by the new workforce. They consider the younger workers lazy, and they struggle with a broadening language barrier. Less engaged than their waiting-for-retirement counterparts, their negative attitude toward the company and management keeps them from offering suggestions for improvement.

The young workers (under 30) are completely surprised when they encounter the negativity and apathy in the older workforce. They have no history that allows them to see the way it used to be. The prevalent negative culture creates a sentiment that literally encourages younger workers to leave the organization.

Veteran workers hoard knowledge like gold, as if this is the only route to respect. Instead, the younger workers become frustrated by this lack of communication. With the lack of guidance in this hoarding environment, they make mistakes that could have easily been avoided with a little direction from the more experienced employees.

The lack of entry-level training means that knowledge transfer is relegated to informal, on-the-job training. This training is inconsistent and often ineffective. Dan's small training budget is scrutinized greatly, and routinely cut in half during budget review. Safety orientation consists of videos and documents to be signed. There is little substance.

Dan was surprised when employee turnover among his younger workers broke 70 percent. With his retiring veterans ,and a slim staff of Generation X, Dan shutters as he looks to the future. He is witnessing the outer bands of the Perfect Storm as it approaches.

**"I say that habit's but a long practice, friend,
and this becomes men's nature in the end"**
~Aristotle

CHAPTER 4

The Least Common Denominator

I have always believed, and often teach, the virtues of hiring the best person for the job. Perhaps naively, I believe that most "right-minded" managers agree with this simple premise. Organizational talent is the foremost indicator of long-term success in the game of business.

I recently experienced something remarkable in my life as a speaker, author, and business coach. It was painful, like a toothache that just would not go away. I tried to ignore the reality of its presence, but simply postponed the inevitable. The existence of this knowledge became something I could no longer ignore. I stirred with this information until I finally had to verbalize my newly formed opinion about the contemporary view of talent in a typical organization.

Like most HR types, I had been boiled (as in the frog and the water) to the point of accepting that we always seek the best talent for the team. I had been certain that most managers agreed with this simple idea. I actually wondered why something so vivid in my own mind was cloudy in the mind of struggling leaders. I could not imagine an organization that didn't want the best talent money could buy. After all, the modern resume and behavioral interviewing techniques, along with testing and personality pro-files, all lead to the very logical conclusion that we are searching for that "one" best candidate to do the job.

And, yes, I really believed the hype..until that day!

That day changed my thinking completely. I was enjoying a relaxing afternoon by the pool of a beau-tiful hotel on the Texas coast. I had spoken that morning at a large convention, and my message was well received by the audience. I was basking both in the sunlight and the success of my work that morning.

I resumed reading the book *Linchpin* by Seth Godin. That book started my figurative toothache.

Since the industrialization of this country one hundred years ago, we have been on a path to find the least common denominator (LCD) in most organizations. In other words, most companies seek employees with the predetermined maximum amount of knowledge and capability that meet the minimum requirement to perform the work. This LCD has resulted in the creation of systems that minimize the need for human excellence, and in some cases human existence.

From the start of mass production, to the robotics and computers of the present, we have slowly become a culture that works very hard to limit our dependence on human talent. In fact, modern manufacturing has so little dependence on the human element that it can be shipped to almost any country in the world where the value of human talent is almost free.

We avoid the extremely talented individuals because they are more expensive, and usually harder to manage. These "Linchpins," as Godin calls them, are often challenging due to their higher level of capability and talent. They know their own value, and are not threatened by the "stick"; instead, they often require a larger "carrot" to perform. We quickly "cull" these candidates as overqualified for the position. We justify the action by stating these people would not stay with the company very long.

Over and over, the typical company looks for any edge that will allow them to hire a less skilled, and often more affordable, employee. Higher turnover, and the generational changes, accelerate this thinking. We use pictures on cash registers so employees don't even need to know how to read to perform their job. We undervalue customer service that we once enjoyed. We have replaced the beauty of the artist with the affordability and predictability of the assembly line. And sadly, we set a budget for wages according to theoretical averages that are based in accounting or industrial engineering, rather than an examination of the potential talent on the team.

I know what you are probably thinking, and you are correct! This is NOT always true. There are companies that do seek and value human talent and creativity. But, you have to honestly admit that these companies are the exception rather than the rule. Finding an organization that places human talent at the core of the competitive advantage is challenging.

Examine your own organization for a moment. Are the front-line employees truly valued, or has the human element become another commodity that can be easily replaced?

Example:

Linda started a company that builds products to fit a specific public need. Her strong engineering background, combined with her belief in the products, resulted in a success. She recruited a highly talented group of leaders to help her run a successful organization with over 80 employees.

The creative products are produced on a mass basis, using technical machines and some basic manual labor. The combination of technology and human interface has placed the organizational focus on improving machine efficiency, and reducing labor costs. Consequently, in the four years the company has been around, the once vital start-up employee population were a budget burden. Attempts to improve profitability became the focus of the entire management team.

An unexpected result slowly and naturally occurred. A perceived devaluation of human worth eroded the promises of great financial success. The focus on unit cost and profitability pushed aside the value of the individual contributor. Most of the original team of 25 are no longer with the company. As a result, Linda is not very close to the new workforce, and her interaction with the front-line employees are limited by the bureaucracy that has developed.

The loss of a competitive starting wage introduced a completely new dynamic to the management team. Supervisors became autocratic and controlling. The employee voice was muffled by marginalization. Linda spent millions of dollars to remove as much work as she could from the employees. The machines now carrying most of the production demands.

The quality of the front-line team member decreased when they began hiring anyone who could pass the mirror test. The joke among managers was that the company would hire anyone passing a drug test and fogging up a mirror with their breath. The company literally sought those who would accept the least amount of pay to support the machines.

The people are kept out of necessity, and the machines are viewed as having more value. Since they are so undervalued, the employees reciprocate with negative sentiments toward the company.

Sadly, Linda knows all this, but she is so busy "running the company" that she conveniently ignores the reality. Worse, not a single person on the team will confront her. The devaluation of the human element has occurred and the new generation of workers will not be a good fit for her company.

"The only thing more expensive than
education is ignorance."
~Benjamin Franklin

CHAPTER 5
The Facebook Future

Almost twenty years ago, the president of the company I worked for made the statement, "If I catch any of my managers wasting time on a computer, I will fire them!" I can still recall the days of memorandums as the primary form of internal business communication. Wow, so much has changed so fast.

Email and Outlook or similar platforms, along with internet, are the foundations for organizational communication today. The next generation of managers will never know any other methodology to communicate. But, could there be another huge paradigm shift that is happening so slowly that we do not readily acknowledge its existence? Could we be seeing yet another major communication shift as we speak?

Most managers and employees that I interview quickly admit (off the record) they check their Facebook page before they check company email. The only exception is when they have Facebook live on their mobile device.

The current perception of Facebook in the business world is that it wastes time. This sentiment sounds like my bosses attitude toward computers all those years ago. The concept of time is evolving, and we are experiencing a major shift in how work is measured. That being said, Facebook could be the next iteration in the constantly changing world of communication. Today, I actually have business contacts who respond faster to Facebook messages than traditional company email.

Smart phones have platforms to support the demand for access to Facebook. This quick-hit message system requires only a data package and quick download from the internet. With the buzz about corporate email security and control, younger managers use the traditional email medium as a last resort. What does this mean for the future of communication?

While only speculation at this point, the trends reveal some interesting possibilities for the future. The internet as we know it will most likely remain as the information super highway; however, the vehicles we use to travel it will certainly change. Traditional websites are already dinosaurs awaiting extinction. Companies that resist the enormous demand for Facebook will break under the pressure. Attempts to control or limit mobile device usage in the workplace will be the losing battle. Progressive thinking leaders will see the potential for better communication through such media as Facebook.

The best explanation for the modern mind set is simply to go where the people are, in order to get them the message you want them to hear. If they are already going to be on Facebook, then that is the best place to communicate with them. This works for all organizational stakeholders, from suppliers, to employees, to customers.

Unless another major change takes place, the most likely method to communicate with others in business is going to be through Facebook. A quick message to someone you have built rapport with by commenting on their profile will be the norm. The clearly defined lines between business and personal lives have already blurred.

Companies have an official Facebook presence that may or may not be linked to personal accounts. They approach "friends" on Facebook, and they request to be "liked." It simply doesn't make sense to ignore this potential.

While your boss may not see all your personal photos on Facebook, it does mean that your ability to "like" or "follow" a business will give mutually acceptable parameters for what is seen, and not seen.

The delicate balance between personal and business will also evolve as the business world enters the Facebook era. Both sides will have to agree to honor the boundaries of the new electronic relationships. Ignoring the boundaries will simply get you "unliked," and you will close the communication portal.

Social media will evolve to the point that it is no longer considered "a" way of doing business; it will become "the" way. Marketing savvy companies like Disney are already exploiting the vast potential for Facebook. Free access to millions of current and future customers is a no brainer. Failing to understand the Facebook potential is like making "buggy whips" or "typewriters" in the modern era. We are seeing the beginning of the end. Companies that do not embrace the potential for social media, will face the end of their relevance in the market.

Example:
Allen started a financial services firm over 28 years ago. That company has grown to over 25 full-time employees, as well as a hand full of temporary workers and interns. The growth resulted from his good reputation and hard work. Four managers have been with him since the early days, and he depends on them greatly.

Most of Allen's employees are under 30 years old, and he is totally confused by the lack of loyalty, as well as the work ethic, of younger workers. He is frustrated by the lack of appreciation, and the pre-occupation with technology and social media. Allen is very "tech savvy," and always buys the latest, greatest gadget for his business. He is connected on social media, but still cannot figure out the younger generation's extreme need to be connected.

As a result, his four managers constantly challenge the younger generation to stop using mobile phones at work. Collectively, the management team considers this activity a waste of time, similar to stealing from the company.

Additionally, Allen spent a good bit of money to remove access to websites like Facebook from the server. Unfortunately, most of the young workers have access to the same sites on their mobile devices. He is considering disallowing mobile phone use in the workplace, but can he set a good example for his team?

Fortunately, Allen had an epiphany! He decided to try something completely different. Instead of resisting technology, and the change it is bringing to the workplace, he decided to embrace it. Instead of banning phones and blocking sites like Facebook, he decided to use the technology to his advantage. Instead of paddling upstream, he turned downstream to enjoy a faster and easier pace.

He assigned daily text message blast responsibilities to each of his managers. The texts to employees were to be quick, witty, and humorous (Twitter style). They were to promote core values, such as customer service and teamwork. He bought a special software package to make the text messaging simple.

Allen even went so far as to create a corporate Facebook page. He continues to make daily posts to the page in a way that connects with other social media sites. His customers see his messages on Facebook, thus visiting his Facebook page and website more often.

Allen's approach focuses on output, and not on time. If the team meets work objectives, he is less concerned about phone usage. He addresses employees who do not meet objectives, but does not worry when people are on the phone or on Facebook. His people are happy and less stressed. Work is fun, and, wow, his workplace is more productive!

Allen knows he will attract and keep the best of the new generation of American workers. Allen gets it!

45

"Success is the ability to go from one failure to another with no loss of enthusiasm."
~*Winston Churchill*

CHAPTER 6
Making the Team

There is something special about the challenge young people face when attempting to make the team. This healthy competition ignites a desire to perform that cannot easily be replicated. Regardless of the sport, the desire to achieve is a remarkable source of motivation.

Imagine the potential if an organization could replicate this motivation on the job. What would happen to key organizational metrics like attendance and productivity?

This current generation of Americans has been labeled as lazy and unproductive. Modern managers cannot seem to tap the potential offered by the smartest generation of workers to date. Previous generations were motivated by the need to get the "good" job. Parents living through the great depression made getting the "right" job the prize.

Today these carrots no longer exist, and the new generation has difficulty placing a job at the focal point of life. The social side of life holds far greater value. The evidence exists in the connectivity, and the need to broadcast life's simplest activities on networks like Facebook and YouTube.

The difference for young workers may seem subtle, yet the results in the workplace are vast. If the job seems menial, or has little personal value, its significance is comparable to a trip to the dentist. It's a necessary and unpleasant activity that must be accomplished. On the other hand, if we can create value in the activity, the desire to perform can change dramatically.

The feeling of making something special holds the key to attracting and keeping the best young talent. After all, if we undervalue their contribution, why would they consider the job to have value? To this point, business has worked very hard to devalue human talent. Why should we be surprised when the "job" holds no importance to the worker?

If a position in your organization is difficult to achieve, young workers will be attracted. Thus, the elevation of young workers, rather than their devaluation, is the first key to success in the new talent game. Creating a workplace to attract these best workers, and selecting only the best workers, will change your organizational paradigm.

And, even more amazing is the effort these workers exert to make your team. If there is no value in being on the team, you will not retain the best. Treating your players like pawns begets more pawns, while treating them like your "queen" attracts more queens. Who you are attracting, and how you are treating them, are the keys to success.

Example:

Tina knows the lines between work and social life are now blurred. As a very smart, 27 year-old entrepreneur, she wants to run her company like no other. She believes she can create a work environment that is productive and effective without giving up the social feeling she gets away from work.

Her company is more like a sorority than a typical dress shop. Tina makes and sells very hip party dresses to the "20 something" crowd in Dallas, Texas. Her unique blend of Texas cowgirl and New York City has caught the eye of several large company buyers. As a result, she now has nine dress makers, three retailers, and two full-time marketing members on her team. Including herself, that is fifteen family members she feels a responsibility to make successful.

She pays her people extremely well. Her wages are almost double the average. She hires fun, sassy people who are a ton of fun. Her small factory and dress shop are open almost 24 hours a day. It has become the hot spot hang out in the neighborhood. She and her team work very hard, but they play very hard as well. As a result, she is bombarded with people wanting to work for her small company.

The team has great autonomy. Each person must meet a weekly production goal based on demand and orders. Working hard is not optional, but somehow they enjoy the pressure of the production schedule. If one person is down, the others pick them up to meet the corporate goal. They get to share in the profits on each dress, and once they are ahead of goal, they can make the same or unique versions for themselves.

These hip young people are the talk of town, and Tina has almost made a local celebrity of each team member in the local media market. She leverages the unique abilities of each person in company brochures, billboard campaigns, and television spots. Her own attitude is contagious, and her team members love her dearly. She professes the team as the source of her inspiration and success. They, in turn, praise her as the bond that holds everything together.

Tina's informal approach and strong accountability are being studied as a model for other businesses. Analysts report that her unusual social environment is attractive to young workers. The single mothers on Tina's team get help with day care, and are offered flexibility when needed. The two married team members are never asked to give up one part of life for another. Tina understands that work/life balance does not work. She believes in, and attempts to foster, a blended approach to work and life. She believes that if passion in work exists, the lines must be difficult, if not impossible, to distinguish.

**"Learn from yesterday, live for today,
hope for tomorrow."**
~ Albert Einstein

CHAPTER 7
Are We Entitled?

What exactly are we entitled to in life? Is entitlement a good thing? The word *entitle* is defined as "to give (a person or thing) a title, right, or claim to something." Can a sense of entitlement create mediocrity?

Let's dig a bit deeper. What exactly do I have a right to? Our American heritage is based upon "unalienable rights" or sovereign rights, of life, liberty, and the pursuit of happiness. I have a right to live, be free, and attempt to be happy. Once we pass these basic rights, it starts to get complicated for most of us.

As a parent of two boys, I am always examining and learning (as if I were never a child or a teenager myself) what motivates positive activities, and what promotes less value-added ways. It is amazing how the purity of childhood is a microcosm for life as adults.

Why do some wealthy parents decide not to leave money to children and grandchildren? Don't the children have a "right" to the money? Aren't they entitled? What wisdom do these parents see in not giving children what many consider to be an entitlement? As parents, we are all guilty of giving too much and creating the "spoiled child" who believes he or she is entitled to the fruits of our labor. Yet, how much is too much or too little?

From labor and effort, we derive appreciation. Conversely, when we derive gain without effort, value begins to diminish sharply. It is only natural to cherish the rare, and take the abundant for granted. While giving is a tremendous human condition, and something that should never be undervalued. It only derives a small amount of benefit for the receiver.

While traveling in a foreign country, I saw almost new "free government" homes virtually destroyed because the tenants had nothing invested in them. Teenagers who invest money in tires are less likely to waste the rubber on the road. Great leaders understand an old yet simple truth, it is much better to teach someone to fish, rather than to give them a fish.

Application of this basic truth can contribute to tremendous growth. When we are shown the path toward excellence, and invest to achieve it, we appreciate the outcome. Simply giving an employee a raise is a very temporary emotional peak. Being entitled to a job based on seniority doesn't require great performance. Keeping a job because you were hired first limits excellence and reduces the drive to deliver. Being too comfortable doesn't require improved performance.

Creating a meritocracy that rewards excellence will transform the organization, and place performance ahead of entitlement. Making a deliberate effort to emphasize effort (leading indicator) will result in more of what you want to accomplish (trailing indicator) for your team. Understanding the difference can transform your organization.

Example:

Rex owns a construction company that has done very well in the past. However, the tough economy has taken a toll on the Rex's company. Through self-examination, and with the help of a good business coach, he is attempting to resurrect his struggling business.

Rex used to hire his employees through the local union, based on seniority. He has even become friends with many of the skilled workers he hires on a regular basis. However, he is struggling to get jobs and remain profitable. Each time he bids a job to accommodate wages, he fails to get the contract. When he lowers his bid to get the contract, he ends up losing money. He is stuck and does not know how to get out of the ditch.

Rex decided he could not correct the problems on his own. He decided to hire Evan. Evan is the business coach who helped his friend, Tom, improve his business. Rex is reluctant to open his company to someone he doesn't know, but decided that he needed the assistance. Pride, and our reluctance to admit needing help, can be a formidable barrier to improvement.

With Evan's help, Rex quickly realized that many of his paradigms are filled with opportunities for improvement. Over the years, Rex has taken for granted the source of workers. With some tough coaching, he now realizes that a temporary worker will probably never care how his business is performing. He realized that some workers may feel entitled to be on his jobs.

Rex decided to slowly change his approach. He began hiring on merit and performance. Loyalty and friendship are great things that should never be under appreciated; however, only one thing gets a job done: performance.

High expectations for performance are now Rex's competitive advantage. He hires only the best, and pays them well. He now pays bonuses to those who finish early. Amazingly, Rex's jobs have become the jobs of choice for local contractors because they move faster, stay on time, and produce less rework. Even more amazing is the fact that Rex has become inundated with business as his reputation for quality grows.

And yes, there has been resistance. People who felt entitled have become angry with him. They have attempted to influence him back to the model of the past. Yet, he is unwavering in his resolve to hire and pay on merit and performance. Rex realizes that the future success of his business enterprise is directly related to the quality of the person he hires. There are no shortcuts for top performance.

"He who speaks without modesty will find it difficult to make his words good."
~Confucius

CHAPTER 8

Enough Leadership Already!

Iknow, I know. There are a plethora of books and articles that point us in the direction of solving our problems with someone else's version of leadership. As a contributor to contemporary leadership principles, I too get caught up in the hype of the next thing. I am often distracted by some very basic truths. Simply put, without the "right" people on the team, the quantity and quality of the leadership provided will always be limited.

That's right, unless we are maximizing our attraction and retention of the human element, the efficacy of the organization is limited. We certainly can improve the performance of our human asset;

however, we cannot compensate for the lack of human talent.

With the high rate of litigation in today's business environment, too many organizations are playing with the talent they are blessed (or cursed) with. They are afraid to make changes because of turnover costs, or the potential for an employee lawsuit.

This environment has created a need for leadership that condones a fear-based culture. Great leadership and paralyzing fear cannot coexist. A cautious approach to hiring and firing limits the performance of a team. Shedding the under-performers and poor attitudes expeditiously helps speed an organization's success.

Risk is commensurate with return. The less risk you tolerate, the less return your team will experience. In the name of risk avoidance, your human element value will become diluted to the point that you longer have the competitive edge. The latent potential of your team will become larger and performance will deteriorate over time. The team will slowly acclimate to the lower standard, which will become the new normal.

Leadership that promotes talent will have a competitive advantage. With the right mix of people, along with their individual capabilities, objectives will be accomplished with relative ease.

With these advantages, why don't more companies not "get it"? In his book *Linchpin*, Seth Godin describes the tendency of organizations to avoid the most talented players. In fact, he states that organizations have become conditioned (since industrialization) to seek the lowest adequate performer that money can buy. The minimum human element quotient leads to a smaller payroll cost. And, payroll is often one of the highest costs in business.

Godin postulates that companies see "linchpins" as those people with the most talent and capability. They appear hard to manage, take more risks, and are expensive (they usually are). These companies would much rather invest in technology than talent.

If your leadership team does not place people and talent acquisition as the core of the strategic plan, your employees may be infected with mediocrity. Attracting and retaining the very best, while liberating the "sub performer," is your key to success. Your business is only as good as the talent on the team—no strategy, plan, or great leadership will compensate for a lack of capability. You just can't fake it until you make it!

Example:

Nancy was hired to run a small oil field operation with about 80 employees on her team. Her qualifications perfectly suited the role of operations manager. She was proud of her accomplishments, and understood the growing demand for technology in the energy business. She worked hard for her

Master's degree in chemical engineering, and she was confident in her five years experience in the oil field.

Nancy also understood that the rules of the game are changing. The paradigm about the "oil patch" was about to change. The reliance on technicians and technology is replacing the traditional "tough guy" image. Training and systems give a competitive edge. Those companies that do not adapt will be naturally selected for extinction by the market.

As a lifelong learner, Nancy saw the critical need for learning in the oil field. She knew the new worker will not learn in the same manner as the worker of the past. She understood that transfer of knowledge from the older workers to the younger workers would be a challenge. Add to that the need to teach the older worker the technology of the present and future, and Nancy faced a significant challenge.

Nancy determined that the entire industry is virtually clueless about formal learning, and the systems required to gain the most return from every training dollar. Informal on-the-job training has been the only system utilized by most leaders. Critical energy processes, and the science to support these competencies, are missing. Nancy knew maintenance, corrosion science, pressure, chemistry and mechanical operations will be the basis of knowledge for even the entry level worker of the future.

Training is usually cut first when it is needed the most. When things recover (as they always do) there is no one capable of operating the complicated equipment properly.

Nancy unlocked the key to the puzzle. The right people are the solution to the challenges most energy companies face. Her complicated industry must attract, develop, and retain the very best. A robust learning and development model allows her to accomplish this goal. She must extract the knowledge of experienced workers before they disappear from the workforce. This core knowledge, combined with the technology of the future, is her secret weapon for success.

Nancy needed to change the current limited corporate understanding in order to gain the sizable budget needed to be successful. She understood that technology can help her accelerate learning, and help her capture existing knowledge. Computer-based learning systems, along with professional training development experts, are the linchpins in the learning process of the future. The access and mobility of this learning is paramount to the needs of the new global worker. Repeatability and demonstrability of competencies through simulation and application will increase learning retention to her goal of 80 percent.

Nancy was initially hired because she has a vision for the oil field of the future. At age 29, she was the high potential candidate for more responsibility. Someday, Nancy may actually run the company, as long as she doesn't leave the company.

"Emancipate yourselves from mental slavery, none but ourselves can free our minds!"
~Bob Marley

CHAPTER 9

Hunger Pains

Can mediocrity dull the hunger pains for excellence? Staying hungry for that which provides the most benefit is extremely challenging and often illusive. Unfortunately, there are many factors contributing to a loss of hunger.

Finding success can be your enemy. This may sound crazy, but marginal success can literally dull the pains that drive us toward excellence.

This phenomenon existed just prior to recent recession. The robust economy created such abundance that business did not have to be excellent to succeed. Poor leadership and marginal management could not dampen the enormous opportunity the economy presented. With success, companies lost the drive to overcome organizational inertia.

Predictably, the first economic challenge put these organizations "out of our misery." The fundamentals of hard work and determination to improve are absolute for long term success in a competitive market. After all, unhealthy food can kill the same hunger that healthy food does. The difference is long-term health.

A recent *USA Today* survey revealed that 50% of companies plan to promote the best talent to keep them on the team as the economy recovers. Nearly half (48%) stated they would raise salaries as the primary strategy to keep key players. The painful truth is that most companies have NO PLAN or strategy to keep the best and the brightest. Some companies take their people for granted, while spending little to nothing on the development of the same talent. This attitude permeates the organization with mediocrity because no one is required to constantly improve performance. Over time, people can literally feel "entitled" to their job, and get comfortable to the point of complacency.

A lack of employee development creates mediocrity that will not survive crises. Failing to have a robust learning effort creates an environment where people become "comfortable," and are not challenged to grow and improve. Mediocre companies cannot afford to train, while winning organizations understand that learning is a mandatory part of the business model for success. Doing more with less requires capable team members with the talent and flexibility to remove the barriers created by the "not my job" attitude.

Consider the big fish in the little pond analogy. The fish can have whatever it wants. There is no one to challenge its place in the environment. Daily, it feeds on the little fish, and gets slow and fat. Days and nights of comfort, and a lack of any threat, makes the fish seem successful. The smaller fish may even envy the big fish and the status it occupies in the small pond. One day, the rains start, and don't stop. The land is flooded, and the big fish is part of a lake many times larger than the original pond. Suddenly and quickly, the fish finds itself in an environment with much larger and physically superior fish. Not long after the flood and the change of status, the fish is consumed and made part of the environment.

Many companies and employees are like the fish. A perceived lack of threat creates apathy that makes people comfortable. Therefore, a safe environment can be a significant challenge facing a mediocre team.

What drives the hunger for success in life? How does this hunger fade as success enters our lives? The true challenge for any successful leader is to create an environment that pushes employees to their capability, and then just a bit further. This challenge is often neglected because managers are not taught how far they can push the talent on their team. This ignorance leads to inaction, and the organization starts to settle.

But there is good news here. Just as coaches and teachers pushed us in the past, we can seek similar pushes in the future. This is why an executive without a coach may become the exception. Being pushed is sometimes the only way to stay hungry!

Example:

Ernest grew up in the late sixties. His aversion to change is rooted in a childhood that moved him every three years. He now prefers consistency, and finds comfort in the feeling that things will be the same tomorrow as they are today.

Ernest started a machine shop fifteen years ago, and because of his great personality, he has grown the business though relationships. He currently employs over 50 full-time employees. The initial investment he made to start the company has been repaid, and he is doing well financially.

But his personal wealth and current business success have become a significant challenge.

The workforce Ernest employs and pays very well averages 57 years old. The equipment he purchased used when he started the business is now out of date. His turnover is low, and he can fix the equipment when it fails. All is well in his mind, and in the minds of his team.

In actuality, Ernest has many challenges that he completely ignores to avoid change. Most of his workforce will retire in the next ten years. A new and modern machine shop is under construction nearby, and his customers are getting concerned about the rising prices Ernest must charge to cover growing salary demands of his experienced machinists.

Ernest has not changed much about his business, and has convinced himself that his current trajectory for business is ideal. His competitor, on the other hand, is hungry. Their focus is technology and flexibility, with a plan to target the best talent from the younger generation. While not able to compete with the hourly wages of the experienced machinists that Ernest employs, the new company prefers, and actually targets, the 25 to 30 year old machinist. These hard to find and highly skilled young machinists are technology savvy and quick to learn.

While lacking experience, the high-energy younger worker is hungry for information. Ernest's competitor leverages learning and information, along with an extremely different approach to the traditional machine shop. This company does not pay by the hour; instead, they pay by a modified profit margin split on every part machined. With this meritocracy, young machinists can work whenever they choose within the deadlines created by customer demand. They are held accountable for tracking key metrics, and having the part ready by the deadline. They can come in early, stay late, work days or nights. The workplace is new, bright and full of energy.

Ernest does not stand a chance with these workers, and the population of older, more experienced machinists is dwindling by the day. The next ten years will be a challenge to survive for Ernest's company. Do you think he will make it?

Hunger Pains

"**Strength does not come from physical capacity. It comes from an indomitable will.**"
~Mahatma Gandhi

CHAPTER 10

The Little Brother Syndrome

As the father of two boys almost eight years apart, I have observed some amazing things about struggle and challenge. While not unique to my children, something strange and positive occurs when a child matches the abilities of an older sibling.

Does the innate competition that drives a smaller child to excel in the presence of a larger, stronger, and more skilled sibling apply to the workplace? Consider the exhaustive effort a smaller child will exert in order to keep up.

Whatever your definition of success, the challenge of "playing up" can make you better at what you do. A common tendency as we age is to take the easy path and justify it as having reached our own potential. This creates comfort, confidence, and, eventual, apathy about personal growth.

Shared mediocrity becomes a crutch, as people become gloriously average among their peers. They avoid the pressure of the shadow cast by greatness. They settle into the role of being hidden by the masses. Invisibility shelters from comparison with excellence.

This is something the "little brother" cannot, and often will not, accept. Being anonymous among billions of humans is not an option to the small child. He will be anything and everything his imagination allows. He will play professional baseball, football, and basketball (at the same time), while working as a police office and fire fighter. No one can tell him he cannot do it all. He knows he can be the superhero. He hasn't been infected with the limited potential that life will saddle upon his shoulders.

When we adopt the mind-set of the small, our capacity for success can be almost infinite. Pain, struggle, and unbridled effort, in the wake of someone we look up to, can make us much better and stronger. Shedding the weight of all the people who tell us "we can't," and forgetting mediocrity, can free our hearts and minds for enormous potential.

Has the smaller size of the American family become an incubator for mediocrity in modern society? In other words, can less competition and more entitlement limit the need to compete for success?

Has the smaller family unit created a generation of Americans who believe that extraordinary effort is not a necessary struggle in life? The lack of siblings limits competition for attention as well as time in the "limelight." Today's young adults have been raised in a period of high prosperity. This abundance may contribute to a lack of hard work.

Find your big brother and chase the same excellence. Delete the comfort of those who make you complacent. Live like a "little brother," and watch your life success grow!

Example:

Lester has worked as a draftsman for the last eight years. He is 34, and has two small children under the age of 4 years old. His wife, Lisa, is a stay at home mother, and the budget is tight.

Lester's boss is a good person with a pessimistic view, and Lester has become accustomed to a doom-and-gloom outlook on life. Lester has slowly become infected by the negativity, and has even started to mimic it.

Lester has tremendous talent, and he is social and outgoing. When he was younger, people told him he would make a great salesman one day. Truthfully, the rare combination of drafting talent and his personality would have made him successful as an entrepreneur.

However, Lester often repeats the negative view that he receives from his boss. He has become boiled (like the frog) to think that he can never make it as a small business owner. He has convinced himself that the responsibility of life is to keep the safe job with the larger company. He must keep the perception of security and stability to protect two small children and a living.

Lester has a good bit of savings and his financial obligations are very small. A modest mortgage and one automobile payment are his only major bills. Lester has both the personality and talent to do very well; however, his negative environment has placed a severe strain on his confidence. Will he take or miss the opportunity?

Lester's plight is common for many aspiring entrepreneurs. The environment that we are in contributes greatly to our confidence to take risks. Choosing to remain in a negative environment (that may seem comfortable) will always have a negative, long-term impact on our life. We are extremely adaptable to any environment, and cannot exist without having a reciprocal influence on us as well. The symbiotic nature of humanity is truly amazing!

The Little Brother Syndrome

**"A matter that becomes clear
ceases to concern us"**
~ Friedrich Nietzsche

CHAPTER 11
Why a Talent Strategy?

If your company lacks a documented, active talent strategy, you will soon spend significantly to attract new employees to replace your empty chairs! Without a viable strategy to keep the best and brightest, your top performers will be easily taken by other companies.

Following are the five major components of an effective talent strategy:

1. **Identify and clarify your true values**. Hanging posters on a wall is not enough! Proactive companies develop a formal communication strategy to perpetually communicate values to all employees. The discipline to create a redundant message is necessary to drive decisions on the front line.

2. **Constantly improve your team's capability to be successful**. Training to practice excellence is critical. Investing in the individual is imperative to long-term success. Employees need training to create the "muscle memory" to perform when introduced to stress on the job. Without training, the response is often what has been practiced most in the past. This simple understanding explains why leaders can say one thing, and do the opposite under stress.

3. **Measure performance and give constant feedback**. Abandon the prehistoric annual performance review for a monthly process that is easy and meaningful. Amazingly, after surveying hundreds of companies and thousands of employees, not ONE is proud of the formal methodology for delivering feedback. Some are tolerant, while others absolutely loathe the annual performance review process.

4. **Funnel business improvement information to employees daily**. The more you include employees in every day challenges and success, the more they will feel like they belong on the team. Think "internal marketing," and you are on the right track! You have to constantly sell the company to your employees. Employees must believe the

hype in order to behave in ways that support business objectives.

5. **Align people with positions based on talent**. You must determine individual talent formally. Do not assume the employee is in the best position on the team. Using a formal methodology to evaluate talent can be very meaningful for your team. Additionally, the role they "want" may not be the "best" role for the organization. Employees get comfortable in roles that allow mediocrity. The fear of change is greater than the fear of failure.

An effective talent strategy cannot be informal or a latent issue hidden within the many roles of the human resources function. Key executive engagement is absolutely critical for the process to be successful. World-class organizations view talent as the linchpin for overall performance. Unfortunately, most companies do not see the competitive advantage potential, and will be reactive as the employment market evolves over the next few months.

The changing landscape in business is going to reveal some strange adaptations in the future of the American business enterprise. A more youthful workforce will most definitely have a significant impact on both the environment as well as the management that occupies the corporate boardroom.

A continual examination of the workplace over the next five to ten years produces some interesting potential for those aspiring to occupy leadership positions. As the workforce becomes younger and younger, the confidence of older leaders may erode as they take a minority position. Combine workplace changes with societal adaptations on the horizon, and even the most confident leader will become influenced by the pressure of change.

Managers of the future will become more and more technology focused to limit the ridicule of "not getting it" from younger, more adaptive workers. Managers of the future will change the current preoccupation with tradition and appearance. The workplace of the future will be more adaptive to styles as well as accepting of body art and piercings.

These future leaders will also become more sensitive to the demands of the worker away from work. A work-centered manager will not gain respect due to a perception of not living life first. The employees of the next workplace will accomplish necessary tasks as a means to achieve other non-work-related activities.

Amazingly, the manager of the next American worker will become more and more oriented toward the needs of the individual. Talented single parents will not feel ashamed of the need to leave work or arrive later, as long as the output is being accomplished. This significant change will force managers to reexamine compensation. And it will be the end of our preoccupation with the 40 hour work week.

Employers will begin to hire and compensate based on productivity and outcomes, rather than time. Truthfully, time is the least effective method to determine effectiveness on the job. Most informed individuals realize that this tradition of paying for time is in no way a representation of merit on the job.

As organizational leaders, we have simply gone along with the past. The belief that the amount of time you spend on the job is equitable with effectiveness is eroding quickly. While workplaces will certainly not change over night, more and more will create adaptive and innovative methods to reward employees.

So, what do CEOs and turtlenecks have in common?

The workplace will soon be so dominated by youth, many managers will be under tremendous pressure to act, think, and, yes, look younger. Our neck area is one of the most revealing anatomical parts of the body when it comes to judgments of age. The prevalence of young, healthy people in the workplace will make those of us getting a bit older more likely to choose clothing that conceals age. Some may choose a nip and tuck. Others may simply choose the turtleneck.

"Failing forward is the ability to get back up
after you've been knocked down,
learn from your mistake,
and move forward in a better direction."
~John Maxwell

CHAPTER 12

Running on Empty?

Leslie left her job after 18 years for another one that pays about the same.

Raymond left his new job of six months for another that pays 25 cents an hour more with a longer commute.

Sarah is looking for a job in another field because she is tired of the negativity at her current firm.

What do these three have in common? They all did not feel appreciated at work.

How can we get the most from our employees? Appreciation is the number one motivator above money, interesting work, and promotion potential. It's true; we have a critical need to be appreciated on the job, and too many leaders simply won't, or don't know how to, show sincere appreciation.

Being appreciated helps replenish the internal drive we have to self-actualize at work. The competitive need to be successful exists in all of us to varying degrees. Some have an insatiable desire for success, and others are relatively content, but we all need to hear that we are making a difference.

The worst offenders of a lack of appreciation have the mindset that a paycheck is thanks enough for the work an employee has done. This myopic view of the human condition cannot see the vast amounts of productivity that are simply left on the table.

Great leaders understand that sincere appreciation provides the energy needed for employees to exert greater effort. This energy can prevent them from taking the path of least resistance.

We have a "sixth sense" when it comes to sincerity. We are good at discerning the sincere from the insincere. Insincerity has little effect on our energy, and can lead to mistrust. If we detect the slightest hint of insincerity in someone's appreciation, it is worthless to us.

A key component for success is a boss who notices the little things. From a little extra effort on a project, to the deliberate effort to be on-time, everyone is capable of doing more when they want to. And everyone appreciates when their efforts are noticed by their boss.

When taken for granted, the desire to do a superior job starts to deteriorate. This deterioration can be incremental or sudden, depending on the individual. Many of us were taught as children to work hard, and we have a difficult time limiting our output. However, the energy to keep giving will eventually subside. This condition leads to discontentment, and we eventually become unhappy with our work.

Great leaders understand that they must make constant and deliberate investments in the energy of those they are blessed to lead. Simple remarks, given with sincerity, can provide an amazing amount of fuel for effort. While we do not all burn the fuel at the same rate, we all need the fuel. Some of us burn the fuel that provides energy at a higher rate, and need more feedback and appreciation; others use and need less.

People must be taught to give, and then held accountable for, sincere feedback. There are clear skills that anyone can learn to utilize. A dangerous assumption is that we already know how to deliver proper feedback. The truth is many people have never been shown the "How To" and "Not To" of delivering feedback. This condition is starving many organizations of the very fuel they need to energize their organizational engines. This sputtering and gasping limits performance, and costs organizations dearly.

Consider your own environment. Do you feel appreciated at work? Do people notice your hard work and extra effort? Have you stopped going that "extra mile" because nobody seems to care? Imagine the lost potential, and the millions of dollars that are simply wasted, because of the under-appreciated among us.

It is not difficult to give sincere appreciation, yet it is a rare occurrence in the workplace. Struggling leaders avoid the effort, leaving employees feeling like they aren't valued.

This trend of taking the worker for granted is rooted in the myopic leadership period after World War II. At the time, people had vivid memories of the Great Depression with its 25 percent unemployment. People valued any job they could get, and they needed little or no appreciation to stay with an organization for a lifetime. In fact, managers could treat these workers badly, and the workers would simply tolerate the treatment.

The second reality facing these managers was the lack of competition around the world. Without a competitive reality in the global market to pressure improved performance, poor leadership and decreased productivity went unnoticed by most Americans. Our substandard products had no benchmark for quality with other countries. This period of prosperity blinded the best companies of the era and made us fat, arrogant, and lazy when it came to organizational leadership. The disappearance of true leadership was replaced by the stereotypical yelling and screaming manager.

It is not coincidental that "worker unions" emerged and gained significant traction during this period of our history. We had not developed leaders; instead, we had managers who instilled fears and leveled threats. The assumption was that if the worker assimilated to the culture, and towed the company line, they could expect "lifetime employment."

Companies did not appreciate the worker during this period. Not only were they taken for granted, but often they were viewed as less valuable than machinery and buildings. Human capital was at it lowest point since industrialization.

Today, we still see the residual damage of this period for the American worker. Mistrust and personal gain are prevalent in many mature companies. Older employees may even carry figurative scar tissue from the wounds of the past. Moreover, as the younger generations enter the workplace by the millions, the remaining older workers cannot imagine the arrogance, and sometimes ignorance, of these young workers. As a result, the older worker withholds valuable information (often gained through experience) from the younger workers.

This withholding of critical information places a significant amount of strain on the knowledge transfer required to continue the operation of any organization. The divide between those with experience and those seeking information becomes greater, and is usually accompanied by a large amount of resentment from both parties.

The result of this divide is what we commonly refer to as the generation gap among members of the team. Individuals occupying leadership positions must be provided critical skills to negotiate the challenges that coincide with this "gap." Further deterioration of relationships will certainly occur when this phenomenon is ignored. Consequently, the erosion of older workers, and the experience they have developed, will become more prevalent as the younger generation assumes more leadership roles.

This situation is not completely negative since it will require the younger generation to learn and adapt to challenges. However, the cost to the organization to "relearn" important details can be expensive, and may even cause some to lose the ultimate battle in a highly competitive environment.

Adaptation to changing markets will certainly require change and speed, instead of size and experience; however, without critical details from the past, some organizations will make large mistakes that will not allow recovery.

Ironically, the very same ignorance that promotes this error will also disguise the pending failure as it approaches. In other words, those in critical leadership positions that are not made aware of, and do not understand, the change, as it approaches. And they will never see it coming. The perfect storm will be upon them before they realize it was in the forecast.

"Blessed is the leader who seeks the best for those he serves."
~Unknown

CHAPTER 13
The Clueless CEO

How can an intelligent and capable executive be so clueless? How can a company be so blind to pending challenges?

While I don't claim to be the next Nostradamus, I do see some remarkable trends that most companies either cannot, or choose not to, see. There can be no other explanation for the blatant apathy. No right-minded, competent executive will ignore these trends if they truly understand the pending impact on their company's bottom line. Yet, over and over, brilliant leaders inform me that they haven't thought about the impact generational trends will have on their company.

Do I think they are stupid, or in over their head? Usually, no. However, I do think some executives consider ignorance as bliss. I believe they see fighting the battles of today as more interesting than planning for inevitable struggles down the road.

The analogy that comes to mind is the hurricane in the Atlantic that is forecasted to hit a large coastal town. Until it gets closer, we are reluctant to plan for the inevitable. These critical trends are so powerful that many companies will be consumed by the challenge presented, and will be oblivious to the forces that will scatter their best and brightest employees. One day, valuable people will just vanish, and the remaining team will struggle greatly with the lack of intellectual capital.

The storm, and all of its power, is modeled accurately through my research and that of others. January 1st, 2008 is a date that came and passed quietly for most companies. The impact of this date will be felt all over the country when the exodus of Baby Boomers is realized. The knowledge they hold will escape the organizations they have worked for all these years. When these storm winds are realized, it will be too late for many organizations to seek shelter.

With 70 percent of our employees disengaged on the job, the current underutilized human capacity is consuming profit margins at an alarming pace. Companies are beginning to hire because they cannot get the same amount of work done. Individual employee productivity will begin to drop dramatically as the pressure of the current recession eases.

The neglected, and mostly absent, "talent strategy" will make it difficult to retain the best employees. They will begin a mass migration not seen in recent times. The people you depend on most will give notice, and you will wonder why you did not see the storm coming.

Organizations do not value learning and information as *the* competitive advantage for the next five years. The maturation of Generation "Y" will compel them to join companies that have a "learning mindset."

The changing values for society are a mirror of the corporate value evolution that is on the horizon. In our working lives, we will see the end of the 40-hour workweek as the standard for work measurement. This antiquated dinosaur will be replaced be a more objective-based measurement system that better quantifies both work output and accountability.

If this information is either alarming or surprising, you need to call a "fast-break time out," and ask these questions of your team. Are you ready for the change? How much will the lack of preparation cost? What will happen if you do nothing?

Example:

Byron runs a historically successful business. His 2,500 employees have seen good times and bad. Business has boomed, and business has gloomed during the company's 25 years. Unfortunately, lately has been more gloom than boom.

The historic predictability of the stock is amazing. Byron has made millions of dollars on stock options as the company moved up and down with the energy sector. He feels very deserving of his spoils.

Yet, his company is struggling to keep pace with changing markets, global pressure, and employee expectations. A strong union has developed over the years, and the huge abyss exists between managers and workers. The wage scale for the employees, as well as the pay for the managers, is good since the main production facility is in a rural part of the country. Unfortunately the ups and downs also created painful and memorable layoffs and reductions in staff.

The cyclical nature of the business has acted as a talent sifter. Tenure is based on union agreements. When labor costs must be reduced to match the business climate, decisions are based on tenure. Every peak and valley creates survivors and victims. Talent has no place on the tenure curve.

Morale is generally bad among the workers, and Byron does not seem to take note. His tunnel vision focuses on profit margin and revenue. He is truly a trailing indicator manager. When the numbers are poor, he reacts negatively with threats of job losses. When the numbers are positive, he is apathetic about those who produce the result. He blames the bad metrics on the performance of the people, and the market gets credit for positive results.

Byron's private plane flies him to the plant, and he flies away without leaving an indelible mark. He does not live in the community that provides the workforce. His expensive home and cars are far from the reality faced by the local team.

The company survives by few talented and battle scarred managers. These leaders have no option other than to manage in an environment dominated by fear and mistrust.

Worse, power comes from institutional knowledge, and it is protected at almost all costs. Employees have learned that the depth of the scalpel (when time to cut jobs) can be minimized by hoarding knowledge.

Byron is not an evil person; he simply does not see the impact of his actions. He is merely replicating behavior he learned. He is not sensitive to the things he does not know, or chooses not to understand. His greed for personal gain has developed slowly.

There are no systems that measure proactively. There are no leading indicators for success. The company is reactive, and looks forward only as far as the next business cycle.

The belief that things will always get better has blinded the executives. The fear of change is so prevalent that leaders dare not express problems in Byron's presence. The very need to improve is an admission of inadequacy among the leadership. Byron has built such a fear in the leadership that most problems are hidden, and work-arounds have been created to mask any hint of problems.

The latest book, or the newest market thinking, is not foreign to Byron's company. However, the application of anything that contradicts the reality of the present is cast aside quickly. Byron believes experts simply do not understand the complexity of his business and market.

The few leaders and risk takers who do make it within voice-range of the executive group are in an awful predicament. They are earning a good living in an environment that does not allow any challenge to the status quo. Even the best leaders are either executed (figuratively of course), or beaten into silent submission. Byron has created an environment that abolishes creativity and learning, and opts for silence and repetition. He truly believes that doing more of the same (only better) is the answer to the challenges of the future.

The problem that Byron cannot see is the change in the American worker. He cannot perceive a workforce that cannot be caught in the web of fear that was spun so effectively with the Baby Boomers. He cannot conceive of an employee who will not put up with abuse. He is clueless about the generation of workers who will not be threatened by his authority, since they do not expect to be around for any significant length of time.

For the first time in his career, Byron is being used by younger workers to make the money, and gain the experience...and he does not realize it is happening.

"An organization's ability to learn, and translate that learning into action rapidly, is the ultimate competitive advantage."
~*Jack Welch*

CHAPTER 14

Why Become a Learning Organization?

How does a learner transform the typical organization from one of mediocrity to a machine of excellence?

The *Harvard Business Review* states that only 10% of people have a learning mindset. These are people who constantly seek out and absorb learning. I call them leading learners.

This means 90% of people will not seek to improve their job skills without a push. They typically must be forced through mandatory continuing education.

Sadly, too many managers view training and education as an interference with work. These myopic managers are quick to cut training and education when the business faces a financial challenge.

In reality, this is the worst time to cut operational expenses. If people are going to be asked to do more with less, training should actually increase. So, why do so many smart managers cut when they should reinforce?

Remember, the leading learner sees, with absolute clarity, the need to train and develop subordinates during tough times. Meanwhile, the average manager (part of the 90%) sees training and development as a cost that must be trimmed in order to maintain profit margin.

Leading learners have a positive view of training and development, and they tend to transfer that same view to subordinates within the learning organization. Meanwhile, typical managers resist training expenditures to the point that subordinates simply will not ask for an investment in learning, unless required. Over time, like-minded managers get promoted, and the organization will evolve toward either the strengths of one or the weaknesses of the other.

Leading learners see change as a requirement for improvement, while typical managers see change as painful. Change and learning are parts of the same thinking that create value in the form of a competitive advantage. Sadly, most managers will not change or seek learning until it is too late, and the competition has already taken advantage of the market opportunity.

Even more amazing is the fact that many organizations invest millions in the least effective form of training without tracking any of the expense. This hidden cost of informal on-the-job training can transfer bad habits, as well as ineffective procedures from one person to another. It creates a climate that devalues training as a collective waste of time and money.

Having Mary watch Tom work until she is ready to try the job on her own will transfer very little knowledge, while costing the organization a significant amount of money. These labor dollars are typically absorbed incorrectly as direct labor because, if they were visible, typical managers would trim these costs as well. The result is a game played by most organizations that perpetuates poor quality training.

Leading learners value effective training. They do not hide costs; instead, they are proud of their investment. In the process, they fine-tune procedures, becoming more efficient and effective. Standards are updated, and quality improves at every metrics. Standardization results in minimized variation, and organizational excellence soon follows.

Quality training is guaranteed to make you money. Human resources become more effective at performing whatever activity you pay them to accomplish. Training reduces turnover, and enables your team to respond to daily challenges. Whether it be customer service, sales, or communication, leading learners know that poor customer service costs a tremendous amount to the organization.

Typical managers, on the other hand, see little or no correlation between learning and business performance. They cannot understand that effective training creates savings.

Leading learners view training and development as a proactive method to continually improve the performance of individuals, departments, and the organization itself. In a world-class learning organization, training and development remain during tough economic times.

If your organization has obliterated training and development in the wake of a challenging economic climate, your fate is more common than rare. The tendency to become myopic or near-sighted when crisis occurs is normal. However, the ability to resist this temptation separates the great from the good.

Example:

Patsy cannot figure why customer service complaints still exist in her business. Her chain of seven restaurants has been successful, but she still receives regular complaints. Her food is very good, but she cannot find good employees.

Patsy's initial training is good (not great), and she pays almost a dollar above minimum wage. She feels her wages are consistent with similar jobs in the food service field, yet she does see more turn-over than she would like.

Patsy does not realize that the content of her training lacks a clear focus on the customer. The training is mechanical, and has a strong emphasis on process. The main focus of her training is "what you should wear," and "what you should do." There is very little about situational customer dynamics; therefore, when employees are in a confrontational situation with a customer, they do not know how to respond. They revert to the mechanical instruction.

This is an example of the "normalcy bias." When Patsy's employees experience stress from a customer interaction, they respond with the normal process training. These employees will actually lose a customer for life over a few pennies.

This is not a judgment regarding the intellectual capacity of her team; instead, it is a realistic depiction of the normalcy bias. When stress is introduced, we seek whatever we determine as normal. In other words, an upset customer will evoke a procedural response from Patsy's employees. This is, after all, exactly (and unknowingly) what she has trained them to do.

In a perfect world, the customer service value that Patsy used to start her first restaurant, would be the basis for the decisions her employees make. After all, she does have posters and lithographs promoting customer service. Her problem is that the managers have been trained to promote the process at the expense of the value. The room for judgment has been intentionally squeezed from daily mental activity. This lack of practice disarms the employees whenever situations occur that are outside the norm.

This lack of clarity around values is confusing Patsy's employees, so they simply opt to act based on mechanical processes. This lack of empathy, combined with the reality of bad customers, created indifference toward customers. The employees stopped making the connection that the customer is the reason for the existence of the company and their job. To make matters even more alarming, when Patsy has to discipline an employee for making a poor customer service decision, the employee often responds with confusion and resentment. They did as they had been trained to do.

These organizational inconsistencies, over time, will cause employees to leave the company. And sadly, when this does occur, Patsy will have no clue as to why the good employees leave.

A lack of quality training will spell the end for Patsy's once successful business. The new generation of employees must have a consistent flow of credible information to remain satisfied on the job. Inconsistency and contradiction will turn away the employees, and Patsy may have to learn this lesson the hard way.

"You are the only person who can label what you do a failure. Failure is subjective."
~John Maxwell

CHAPTER 15
The Power of a Willing Mind

Imagine the impact of a fully engaged workforce on the economy. Consider the productivity and profit that is there for the willing organization to take.

And yet, according to the Gallup organization, only 30% of employees are fully engaged in their work. That means 70% are merely earning a paycheck. What does this cost an organization? And, why are so many companies oblivious to this loss?

I recently checked into a hotel. The parking lot was virtually empty, so one would assume the hotel was equally unoccupied.

Now, I have earned a "platinum" status with this hotel chain from the amount of business I have done with them. At check-in, I asked the young lady if she had my frequent status in the reservation. She stated no, and looked me up. Upon discovering my status, she thanked me for my loyalty. I then asked her if a room upgrade was available. She paused (obviously she did not want to redo the reservation), and politely told me there were no rooms available for upgrade. Knowing this was not true, I politely accepted the room I was offered. After all, I was only staying one night.

But let's explore this example further. At the moment she said "no," a small seed of doubt was planted in my mind. I began to doubt the appreciation she uttered, and I also doubted the appreciation the hotel chain had for my extensive business.

This seed can now grow, or it can be removed by the next contact I have with this particular hotel chain. How many other incidences like this will it take before I switch my loyalty to a competitor? The executives in this organization spend millions to get me (and people like me) to stay at their hotels. Had they been standing there when I checked in, I think the outcome may have been different.

Decision making is easy when values are clear. In other words, employees usually make the best decision based upon their perception of what the company finds valuable.

According to my research, profit, cost-reduction, and productivity are among the most common values perceived by employees. Ironically, stated values are typically concepts like communication, accountability, and customer retention. So what exactly is the source of this disconnect?

Unfortunately, it is the rare company or organization that invests in selling a message to their employees. Large companies target potential customers with millions in advertising dollars, but they spend little selling a message to employees.

When I ask employees what the "main thing" is for their company, the answer is usually vague and inconsistent. In seven years of research with thousands of people, not one company that I have worked with has really done exceptionally well with internal promotion of values.

Imagine the corporate metamorphosis that would occur if untapped employee buy-in were one of the major financials that guide our businesses.

The challenge for internal marketing is no different from external. We have to repeat a message over and over for it to resonate with our audience. Leadership is the mouth piece for values. Through constant action, the message has to become redundant to be effective.

The solution is simple, yet difficult, to attain. If communication is truly a value, employees who value communication must be selected to lead. Results must become a by-product of deliberate effort to achieve excellence. Myopic leaders who seek profitability over process must be de-hired.

Choosing the best people, with values that match the corporate message, is the shortest route to the excellence!

Example:
Charlie started his landscaping business with one mower and one trimmer almost ten years ago. His magnetic personality, combined with a strong work ethic and a keen eye for detail, has gained him a strong customer following. In fact, he now has 15 trucks and over 30 employees. He pays his employees well, and even provides benefits for his full-time employees.

Lately, however, Charlie has noticed that some long-term clients are leaving him for his competition, and he cannot determine the reasons. He has a small amount of turnover, and believes he has the best team available to support his small company.

An examination of his company reveals a different story. Charlie is a loyal person who trusts people. He is optimistic about human nature. Most of his employees are friends, and children of friends. They seem to be hard workers, and generally arrive at work on time.

Charlie's problems are based on the fact that his employees are not Charlie. Many employees are not friendly, and more than a few do not appreciate detail. In fact, most employees feel that the more work they do in a day, the better they are doing for the company. Fast is always better than beautiful.

This small crack in the armor of Charlie's company has created fertile ground for his competition to grow. Accounts that were once impervious to attack are now vulnerable. And Charlie cannot figure out exactly why he is threatened.

Unknowingly, Charlie has hired good, hardworking employees who simply do not share his values for human relationships, or his attention to detail. The reason many clients originally agreed to do business with Charlie is now being contradicted. They want "him," and feel like they have received someone else.

Charlie's employees are going though the motions, and he is too busy to notice. If he isn't careful, Charlie will become just another landscaper to his customers. In this environment, a competitor can lure customers away. Charlie has lost his differentiation in his own market.

"An army of a thousand is easy to find, but, ah, how difficult to find a general."
~ Chinese proverb

CHAPTER 16
Find Out Why,
"I Hate My Job!"

Have you heard these statements?

- As a supervisor, there is nothing I can do about it.

- I accepted this promotion to supervisor because I need to improve things for my family.

- I can't stand confrontation and don't like dealing with other people's problems.

- I don't know what I am doing.

- I haven't received much training, so I'm winging it.

- No one told me that supervision would be like this, and I am not sure what I should do next.

- If I admit the truth, I will be viewed as a failure, and the company will never offer me another opportunity.

- I really liked my "old job," and the company is not a bad place to work.

- I can't see myself doing this job for the rest of my career.

Unfortunately, these comments are common within most organizations. Good people with the capability to perform are promoted to positions that they are not prepared for; worse, they often dislike their new position.

Too often, great employees are made into average, or below average, supervisors. Most companies assume that because the person was good at their job, they will make a good supervisor. Most of the time, this is farthest from the truth.

These under-performers are afraid to admit that they either don't like the new job, or feel overwhelmed by the expectations. This stress causes them to replicate whatever model for supervision that they consider to be successful. In other words, they will simply replicate what is familiar, rather than what is truly effective.

In truth, the transition to a leadership position can be very challenging, and many companies invest little to nothing to encourage success at this critical career point. They simply "hope" the talented individual performs well in the new role. While "hope" is indeed positive, running a vital and successful business requires a bit more effort and investment.

Example:

Nathan was promoted to supervisor almost one year ago. He was an exceptional welder; in fact, that was the main reason he was selected to be supervisor. No other criteria were utilized to promote him.

Unfortunately, Nathan hates his new job. He loathes conflict, and despises dealing with people's problems. The small raise that he received upon promotion is certainly not worth the struggle he feels at work. He used to enjoy coming to work, and now gets physically ill thinking about his next day.

To make matters worse, Nathan feels like he cannot tell anyone how he feels. Management made a big issue when they promoted him, going so far as to suggest he was "management material" for the future. His wife is proud of his new position and the potential for growth he now has at work. His parents often say that he is "going places" at this company.

Still, Nathan secretly hates his new role and responsibilities. He often thinks about the low stress and enjoyment he used to have when he would simply come to work and weld. He does not see a road back to the days when he liked his daily activity. Sadly, he is starting to get used to the new job.

Nathan is not a terrible supervisor, even though he has received no leadership training. He has simply attempted to copy the behavior of other supervisors.

Nathan has not been taught the difference between communication and effective communication. He does not understand the difference between accountability and blame. Trust is not central in his role as a leader. He is winging it, and making many mistakes. While he is indeed learning from these mistakes, the lessons are not always optimal for success. He has no leadership foundation to build upon, and will only become marginally successful, if at all.

The thing that Nathan secretly fears more than anything is that he will continue to do this job, or get promoted to another management job. He is afraid that he is doomed to this new role for the rest of his career. His worst fear is another 20 years of the same thing. He yearns for someone to put him out of his misery. If he could only bear the humiliation of being fired or demoted, he might be happy again. He is too proud to do substandard work, and can never let the people around him down. He ponders when the economy will get bad enough to get laid off.

"Generally speaking, there are two kinds of learning: experience, which is gained from your own mistakes, and wisdom, which is learned from the mistakes of others."
~John Maxwell

CHAPTER 17
Beware the Training Wannabes

In nature, many creatures have copied the characteristics of other, more beneficial organisms. I think of the insects and animals that copy color patterns as wannabees in the natural world.

This phenomenon is not unique to the animal world; in fact, it is common in the world of business. If something is perceived as successful, imitators are quick to appear. And it may be hard to differentiate from the original. We see this in business plans, logos, products, and even training.

The abundance of grants and other funds have created a plethora of training providers in the business community. From non-profits to community groups, it seems everyone is a training provider these days. It is often tough to separate the imitators, just like it can be difficult to see a camouflaged creature in the wild.

Many groups find it valuable to leave the rigor of their competencies, and attempt to provide value in the form of knowledge transfer. Information for a thirsty generation seems to make a great deal of sense. In an economy with people worried, why not offer hope to the struggling enterprise in the form of business or personal growth?

Tragically, these false creatures are common. With little knowledge or experience, with no understanding of knowledge synthesis, these wannabees invade the organizational development market.

Armed with a promise of grant reimbursement, these so-called training providers make claims of excellence to a hopeful and concerned public. Businesses struggling to stay afloat are grabbing at anything they can to survive, and will spend (in some cases what they do not have) in order to gain a glimmer of hope for the future. All the while, these imitators are more than willing to take the last dollar, and make the promise of salvation or transformation.

Warning: These trainers are in disguise. They seem harmless on the surface, and may even offer the hope your team is hungry to achieve. But there are no short-cuts for business excellence.

When you see a great offer, remember you usually get exactly what you pay for. Excellence takes discipline, redundancy, and effort.

Your team can achieve excellence through a commitment to learning that is ongoing and iterative. Each competency builds upon the successful achievement of the past.

Hitting a 90 mile-per-hour fastball cannot be learned in a weekend seminar. That skill is learned over years of development. It requires working with a coach with a foundation of talent. In the same way, great customer service, quality production, or work-safety are all based on cumulative principles that are taught the proper way. Investing in the proper development of your team can truly become a value, and eventually become a core-competency for your organization.

Example:

Ursula managed a small products company in Texas. She has been blessed with a stable workforce and very little turnover. The median age of her 64 employees is 51. Attrition became an issue as more and more employees notified her of their pending retirement. Additionally, the new applicants were younger, and did not bring the same amount of knowledge to the workplace as her retiring staff.

Ursula knew training would become necessary, but she didn't budget for it. She figured that training is training. All you need to do is have someone stand in front of the employees and tell them what they need to know.

Ursula had her administrative person deliver the safety policy statements that described such things as the location of the bathrooms and the organizational chart. Additionally, the most senior operators instructed new employees using traditional, and largely ineffective on-the-job-training. These veteran employees skipped vital details that they had taken. They left out important information that took them years to learn. After all, why should they give that away? Knowledge, after all, is power.

Historically, training was limited at Ursula's company. The financial investment was minimal, and Ursula could not justify a larger investment in something as basic as training employees. She had no idea that ineffective training would cost her company more than the minimal investment in quality training.

Ursula never viewed training as an on-going investment. The concept of redundancy for application has never been a part of the discussion. Accountability, and the methodology to ensure training application, is simply not relevant.

At the time when she needed it the most, the idea of becoming a "learning organization" was totally foreign to Ursula and her team. She selected trainers (internal and external) based on cost; as a result, she saw little benefit from the outlays.

Without training, we can expect new employees to make horrible and preventable mistakes that will cost Ursula's company dearly. Unfortunately, she is too ignorant to connect the root cause back to the capability of her workforce. This lack of skill and knowledge will become a large financial burden on her company as the talent exodus emerges. Ursula will be left blaming the younger workforce as lazy and incompetent.

**"I am more afraid of an army of 100 sheep
led by a lion, than an army of 100 lions
led by a sheep."**
~ Talleyrand

The Myopic Leader

According to the Gallup organization, only 30% of employees are fully engaged in their work. That means 70% are merely earning a paycheck. What does this lack of employee buy-in cost the average financial institution? And, why are so many companies oblivious to this loss?

Imagine the impact of a fully engaged workforce on the economy.

I recently went through the drive-through line at a local bank that I had been considering for my business account. It was after lobby hours, so the drive-through line was my only option. I felt like my request was simple and straight forward. I wanted 100 crisp one-dollar bills for a marketing campaign. I thought I made my request clear to the voice behind the glass. After a few moments, counting the ones I suppose, my envelope arrived via the long tubes. Upon examination, the old bills had folded corners and wrinkles. Quite the opposite of the expectation I had.

I paused, waiting for the voice to say "thank you" or "have a nice day" while pondering how I may have miscommunicated my simple request. The voice never came. I drove off in disgust over how I was treated.

Let us explore this example further. At the moment I viewed my sad little envelope of one-dollar bills, a seed of doubt was planted in my mind as a potential customer. I now doubt the bank will ever make me feel important, and I also doubt the quality of the institution. This seed will now grow each time I tell this story, or drive past the bank. To this day, I have not found the need, nor the desire, to enter that property. It is doubtful I will ever do business with that company.

Of course, the executives spent thousands to attract my business account. Had they been standing there when I made my request, I think the outcome may have been different. But their employee did not have their values, nor did she care whether I became a customer or not.

Decision making is easy when values are clear. In other words, employees will usually make the best decision based upon their perception of what the company finds valuable. Profit, cost-reduction, and productivity are among the most common values perceived by employees. Ironically, the stated values of companies usually run along the line of customer service, accountability, and communication. What is the source of this disconnect?

Unfortunately, it is the rare company that invests in selling a message to their employees. Large companies target potential customers with millions of advertising dollars, but spend little selling to their employees. It is actually humorous when employees tell customers not to believe everything they hear on television.

When I ask employees what the "main thing" is for their company, the answers are always vague and inconsistent. In seven years of research with thousands of people, not one company I've worked with has done exceptionally well with the internal promotion of values. Imagine the corporate metamorphosis that would occur if untapped employee buy-in guided business.

The challenge for internal marketing is no different from external. For instance, we have to repeat a message over and over for it to resonate with our audience. Leadership is the mouth piece for values through constant action. The truly world-class company makes its actions consistent with the message.

Tragically, it is often the lowest paid employees who have the most significant opportunity to sell and keep the best customers. Yet, little is invested in arming them with skills and tools for customer retention. Instead, they are treated like inter-changeable parts that can be replaced with an ad in the local paper.

If customer service is truly a value, employees that value the customer must be selected to lead. Results must become a by-product of deliberate effort to achieve excellence. Myopic leaders who seek profitability over process and methodology must be de-hired. Choosing the best people with values that match the corporate message and vision. Remember that excellence is a journey rather than a destination!

A recent study revealed that the key to human happiness is the ability to live in the moment. Our obsessive preoccupation with the past and the future limits us. Our stress over past events, and worry about the future, have a negative impact on our business. Our need to learn from historical trends or undesirable events causes managers to be preoccupied with blame. Communication becomes filtered, and honesty is rare. Accountability is defined improperly, and trust is scarce.

Additionally, the over speculation about the future can be equally as demoralizing. The emotional strain created by the economic fluctuations can kill morale, and impact current productivity significantly. Wasted organizational energy over possibilities is the "boat anchor" to productivity and profitability.

The answer, though simple in concept, is more challenging in application. The concept of boosting morale to enhance productivity is not revolutionary, yet most companies actually create an environment that limits individual productivity. Many corporate policies have a detrimental impact on the collective happiness of the team. The most demoralizing of all policies are the zero-tolerance policies designed to punish everyone for the negative actions of the few. The fear of corporate litigation (future) coupled with precedent actions (past) lead to an unhappy workforce.

Again, too few companies focus on creating an environment that promotes output. Modern managers are not taught to nurture productivity; instead, they are taught to emphasize results. This misguided emphasis rewards the lucky, and punishes the diligent on the team.

Winning at business is about performance in the present moment. Neglecting the now in order to win later simply has no logical basis. The old cliché still rings true that a happy employee is a productive employee. There are no shortcuts or quick fixes. Your team's happiness holds the key to the success of your business.

Too often, leaders understand the factors that promote productivity, yet still fail to execute at critical opportunities. Why can leaders say (and even believe) the right things, and then contradict the very same with their teams? Why does leadership theory get diluted in application on the job? How can we develop leaders to execute properly?

Most inexperienced leaders can quote the management theory that promotes better followership, but, when stress is introduced, we revert to some basic behavior that may not have a positive long-term impact. Some people change very little when under stress, while others change dramatically. It is this change (great or small) that confuses followers, and minimizes leadership.

The skilled leadership coach can filter the theory, while gaining profound insight that are based on the behavior that has been exhibited in the past. The challenge for most leadership coaches and trainers is the futile effort to replicate stress in the laboratory of a coaching session or classroom.

Simply put, it is virtually impossible to replicate the actual stress faced on the job due to a lack of consequence if failure occurs. Sports are a great example of this phenomenon. A player can execute flawlessly during practice, and then fail miserably during a game. Most golfers would love to replace their actual swing with their practice swing. Batting practice is much easier than facing an opposing pitcher. And believe it or not, shooting free throws in practice is much easier than standing at the line in the last seconds of the game.

The idea of consequences and stress are the most overlooked, yet significant, barriers to effective leadership on the job. The only way to improve as a leader is to create the same muscle memory that we learn in competition. Unfortunately, most people are afraid to apply what they know to be the proper behavior if it requires changing the normal behavior of the past. We will actually do the wrong thing intentionally because we fear the unknown result of a better way of doing something. This may sound preposterous, yet you have seen it over and over with struggling leaders.

The secret to enduring leadership greatness comes with the same success factors that promote excellence in anything else we attempt in life. We must practice with intense frequency until the muscle memory (mentally or physically) predicts our behavior under stress. One leadership class or generic workshop will not change our behavior.

The greatest incubators for leadership are extremely realistic and redundant practice sessions. This reality is evident by the explosion of the leadership coaching market. My executive coaching business has tripled in the last twenty-four months as leaders become proud to have a coach to help them improve.

A skilled leadership coach can create real-life activities that promote changes in behavior under stress. This intensity, combined with significant repetition, accelerates leadership growth. Using situational leadership, along with historical behavior, can amplify the likelihood that someone will practice the principles that support great leadership.

The interruption of leadership is more common than most like to admit. We fail to behave in the manner that is most conducive to leading others. In other words, we may believe we are leading when we are not, and we may be succeeding when we think we are failing. The truth is a constant state of change based on the perceptions of the people we are in contact with.

The best analogy I can think of is a batting average. Whether or not you strikeout (fail) is not the issue; it is the collection of batting attempts, preceded by countless hours of practice, that promotes a likelihood for success. Being willing to work hard allows us to reach our potential. The skills and knowledge we develop determines our capability for leadership success, while being willing to fail allows us to improve.

"Globalization has changed us into a company that searches the world, not just to sell or to source, but to find intellectual capital - the world's best talents and greatest ideas."
~Jack Welch

CHAPTER 19

The Changing Role of Human Resources

What exactly is the role of human resources in today's organization? Have we evolved the function to meet the norms of modern society? Have current societal trends bent the function into something new?

Unfortunately, the most common purpose for modern HR is to prevent litigation. HR has become a localized arm of the corporate legal entity that seems to be more focused on risk reduction, rather than organizational enhancement.

In this environment, leaders become paralyzed by the potential for litigation, rather than tactical and strategic with the human asset. Too many frontline leaders feel stripped of the authority to choose, keep, or de-hire their team because of the inordinate amount of bureaucratic "red tape" they face. Consequently, leaders are helpless to attract the best team members, and they settle for whatever human resource they receive.

Instead of realizing that risk truly does equal return, as we learn in basic economics, we promote mediocrity by inhibiting the changes necessary for better overall performance. At the same time, employees become complacent with underperformance. They feel little or no need to perform at a higher level. The threat of being replaced is so remote that it does not factor into attitude, attendance, and productive output.

Conversely, the exceptional organization seems to be more capable of leveraging the HR function. In these organizations, the HR professional is a key member of both strategic planning and tactical execution of the business plan. These professionals fine tune organizational talent to enhance organizational performance. They are connected to senior management's every action. Talent management becomes the most significant activity for the team.

There is a compelling understanding that profit and share-holder value are a mere by-product of talent. Long-term results are the fruit of capable talent, while short-term results are merely the reflection of poor or diluted organizational talent. These modern organizations are looking five to ten years into the future, while others are looking at who is standing in line at the local employment office.

In reality, many organizations exhibit traits from both descriptions; however, it is impossible to live in both worlds. The balance will always tip in one direction or the other, and the effort to move in the other direction is always "uphill."

The current challenge facing organizations will benefit the talent organization greatly as the recession moves toward recovery. Many organizations are going to be caught in a "musical chairs" event that will accompany pending economic growth. The lack of a clearly defined and implemented "talent strategy" will cripple some organizations as the best and brightest people migrate to better opportunities.

Do not wait; develop and implement your plan today. You have only a few months until the migration begins!

Example:

Miranda was the human resource director for a regional hospital. She was with the company for nearly 15 years. She was good at her job, but somehow her role has changed over the years. Slowly, the primary function of human resources has become more about litigation prevention than human resource enhancement. Miranda felt more like a subordinate of the legal team.

Ideally, Miranda wanted the human resource function to be an internal resource used to field the best players. She knew that having the right talent in key positions is the most effective way to run the hospital. Helping get the right people on the team, and assisting the exit of those that did not work out, should be her focus.

Yet, the leaders in the organization undermined Miranda, so she turned to threats and fear techniques to gain organizational power. Ironically, this was the only way she could be respected by her peer group. She became the "bad guy" that told others what they could and could not do.

Miranda would rather have served as an internal consultant to the leadership team, helping them achieve both tactical and strategic organizational success. In her mind, human resources should be the conduit toward excellence.

If she had her way, she would connect with each key leader to get the right people in the best positions. Each leader should seek her counsel about the successful implementation of the talent strategy. Her team should function more like the talent scout to maximize human capability.

Instead, the other leaders avoid her office. The human resource function became punitive and bureaucratic. Her team became a thorn in the side of the other leaders. She was reduced to use the threat of a lawsuit to get compliance.

There was one case that caused trepidation for Miranda. She did not discuss it out loud because the circumstance was simply too appalling to consider. A minority, female employee in her billing department was an under-performer. She met the minimum criteria to keep her job, but carried a horrible attitude toward others. Her performance and attitude were totally inconsistent. She repeatedly threatened to file suit on the hospital if she were ever terminated. Because she was in two protected classes, according to the human resource profession, the hospital ignored her poor attitude and accepted her minimal performance.

The entire department suffered, and the fear of litigation paralyzed the hospital. It accepted the bad employee as a cost of doing business.

The manager of the billing department felt that what he teaches and promotes for his team was undermined by this one employee.

Deep down, Miranda was ashamed. She knew this manager was correct. She also knew leadership equity was being eroded. And most importantly, she knew she lost the respect of others. Miranda did not know how to unwind the horrible mess she created. Sadly, doing nothing seemed easier than the effort required to remedy the situation.

"Good leaders make people feel that they're at the very heart of things, not at the periphery. Everyone feels that he or she makes a difference to the success of the organization. When that happens people feel centered and that gives their work meaning."
~Warren Bennis

CHAPTER 20
Human Resource Heroes

CEOs come from three functions in most companies: sales, finance, and operations. Ever wonder why so few human resources (HR) executives are chosen to sit in the corner office? Has the position of HR been devalued to an ancillary function on the executive team? If so, how did it get this way?

When Jack Welch took over General Electric in the early 1980s, he transformed the company from a product oriented entity to a people oriented, talent machine. With the nickname "Neutron Jack," he carved away the bureaucratic "fat" to reveal a leaner and meaner performance-based organization.

The transformation made GE a virtual leadership factory, and companies began to select and woo potential talent from the GE school of leadership excellence. Welch knew that talent was the key to organizational performance, and he broke the trends of leadership selection. Though not from the HR function, he made human resources and talent excellence the critical function of the company.

Amidst the success that GE experienced in the next two decades, why didn't more companies copy this view of talent? Why haven't more CEOs come from the HR discipline?

While most CEOs agree that the only real competitive advantage comes from talent, many of them continue to devalue the HR function. Yet, the best and most dynamic companies all agree that the real advantage comes from putting talent at the heart of every business plan and strategy.

It is painful and uncomfortable for me, as a member of the HR function, to admit that too many HR executives have simply "sold out" to the rest of the executive team. They have sacrificed what they know to be true in order to keep a seat at the table of executives.

The typical HR executive gains favor among executive peers by mitigating or avoiding lawsuits. Their short time in the spotlight comes when they discuss how to protect the organization from multi-million dollar litigation. Unfortunately, this euphoria is short-lived. The small piece of the agenda is pushed to the side, meanwhile the real game of competitive business resumes. Organizational strategy and operational excellence take over, and the mandatory HR piece is glazed over with an, "OK thank you, what's next?"

I believe there are HR Heroes out there. These heroes know talent (and its proper deployment) is the true key to organizational success. They believe that the fear of litigation and the formation of more bureaucratic company policy are far down on the list of functional priorities. They believe the formation and execution of a clearly defined and deliberate "talent strategy" is the key function of the entire executive team.

These HR Heroes have influence among the executive team, and support the principle that success comes from "leading" indicators, rather than "trailing" indicators, such as profit margin and revenue. These true leaders are focused on what determines results, rather than the results themselves.

If HR doesn't report to the CEO, or if it doesn't have a seat on the senior executive team, the organization is a dinosaur awaiting extinction. The core of the business strategy for the next five, ten, and fifteen years should be focused on retaining, recruiting, and developing the best team. Engaging senior management requires extreme candor, diplomacy, and above all, a willingness to go "all in" when necessary.

Remember that Peter Drucker said that obsolescence must be planned into products and processes in order to stay ahead of the competition. A company or product that is stagnant creates opportunities for competitors. In other words, your competition will replicate the success you have achieved; therefore, innovation delivers a competitive advantage. HR needs to be a part of this innovation.

HR Heroes develop a culture that mandates innovation in every process and product. This thinking directs hiring decisions as well as promotion. Employees who do not promote innovation should not be promoted, and should not be in leadership positions. Resistance to change should be a disqualifier.

A significant challenge for many organizations is talent complacency. We become complacent with our current talent, and settle for performance mediocrity. We disguise this lack of leadership as loyalty to those who have been employees for a long time. We hide from the leadership role we are supposed to occupy. We abdicate the function of managing the team to attrition in order to make life easier on ourselves. We hide behind the threat of corporate litigation. We become apathetic over the challenge of finding new and better qualified talent.

Thus, we end up with an organization threatened by the competition. Instead of creating a challenge for our competitors, we make it easier for them to beat us at our own game. Worse, the competition picks up the better talent, while we are stuck with ineffective employees.

A professional sports team is a great example of accountability and talent management. Winning the game is the ultimate goal. Loyalty, friendship, and tenure have significantly less influence on the decisions made by managers. This purity of purpose helps clarify decisions at all levels of the organization. Even the most seasoned and accomplished player will admit (albeit with difficulty) when he can no longer perform at the level that benefits the team. Professional quarterbacks that once led the National Football League will accept roles as teachers or mentors to the new talent that can take the team to the next level. This reallocation of talent is very common, and new roles are readily accepted by players.

Business leaders can learn from the performance requirements and expectations of professional sports franchises. Making decisions for the benefit of the collective, even at the expense of the individual, is the norm in sports. Meanwhile, in business, the focus on the individual often surpasses the collective benefit.

Imagine a business that places talent at the pinnacle of the strategic and tactical operation. Every decision should be filtered through the performance and talent of the organization. The result will be better customer service, improved quality products, safer activities, reduced cost, and more profits. Innovation and improvement will become the expectation rather than the occasional surprise. Complacency will be scrutinized and forced out of the organization. Leaders will see the future as something far different than the present. Employees will come to work with the expectation for change. Success will be experienced at all levels of the organization.

"Leaders don't force people to follow—
they invite them on a journey."
~ *Charles S. Lauer*

CHAPTER 21
The Roach Theory

Leaders should be constantly evaluating the talent on the team, yet employee development is one of the most neglected parts of the business model. Instead of spending effort and money on the development of the team they have, many organizations focus resources on recruiting new talent. Does this make sense?

A major reason some executives neglect employee development is that there is simply no place for "human capital" on basic financial statements that govern most businesses. In fact, struggling leaders will often promote people to their level of incompetence by simply allowing "good people" to become supervisors and managers. The sad truth is most companies do not train or prepare people for leadership positions. They leave the failure or success of their leadership to the roll of the dice.

It is amazing that most companies see training and development as a necessary evil, rather than a methodology to create a competitive advantage. Additionally, when times get tough, companies cut the very people who made them successful. If winning the game were the goal, why would we ever get rid of our best players? If we are in the game of business to make a profit, why would we ever eliminate the talent that makes money?

Building a successful bench is not just an option for large companies; it is a necessity for every successful team, whether we are talking about sports or business. In word-class organizations, talent development is an integral part of the business plan. In fact, the best companies are always looking for new and better talent, while they develop the talents of the team they already have.

Developing others for success strengthens the entire organization. For instance, Jack Welch transformed General Electric from a product company to a leadership factory that also made products. Take the example Southwest Airlines. It takes care of employees first, knowing that the employees will take care of the customers.

Some leaders are so nearsighted that they do not realize success is often "indirect." Think of it this way, success in baseball is often preceded by hours of boring practice and so called "silly" drills. The success comes not from the moment at the plate, but from the cumulative effort of the past. Muscle memory takes over, and the batter hits the ball with what looks like very little effort.

In the game of business, when do you get to practice? Training and development are the practice opportunities in business. While not a guarantee for success, the preparation makes success much more likely when challenges arise.

For lack of a better analogy, the following observation is called the "Roach Theory" for leadership and development. The Roach Theory states: "Leaders who need leadership training the least want it the most, and those who need it the most want it the least."

When exposed to the principles of leadership, communication, accountability, and trust, bad leaders avoid the conversation like a roach avoids the light. Leaders who do not practice communication, accountability, and trust want to change the conversation or conclude the meeting. Conversely, the best leaders are always learning better ways to improve how they influence and direct the actions of others.

In order to grow, we must study and not be ashamed of our current lack of knowledge. When we are ready to admit the need for growth, we begin to add value to the team. Learning should be a pleasure, while studying should become a discipline by which we manage the organization at every level.

Learning should be both a science and an art. In other words, there are things that are shared by all people (science), and there are talents unique to each individual (art). Great leaders understand this simple truth, and manage the capability of the team accordingly.

To begin the journey of self-growth, we must first identify the direction we want to go. Information and perspective is not always the same for the receiver as it was intended by the transmitter. Remember the fact that your team members can have different filters to the same information, and may not arrive at the same conclusion that you expected. While translations of information are unique to the individual, they can be guided by the organizational leader.

When developing your team, remember that they may not absorb the same information at the same rate, and they certainly may not arrive at the same interpretations. Our personal biases will fragment the information. The most effective learning for the team will be accomplished in an environment that is open to challenge and discussion. The long-term result is a team that is willing to disagree, and still support each other when challenges arise.

The most effective method for creating a positive learning experience is to explore the most common knowledge, and then build complexity from that point forward. If the young leader does not make a connection, the information will not be retained. Moreover, the best development occurs through a hybrid of instruction and encouragement. This balance over time will make the learning seem more organic, and it will be accepted more readily.

Each team member must be developed to ask key questions in order to accept the information being presented to them. Following are the four critical questions that each student on your team must be willing to ask:

1. Who is the source of the information, and does it make a difference?

2. What is the underlying message or key point from the information?

3. When was the information developed, and does it make a difference today?

4. Why is the information valuable, and how has it been able to remain applicable in today's business climate?

Students of leadership should be challenged to ask how the information will be valuable to them and the work they perform. This simple relevance "hook" will promote more retention, and the employee will be more likely to apply the learning on the job. Teach the learner to determine what they derive from the information.

Additionally, the best way to learn is to teach others. Learning to teach creates a strong process for retention in our minds. The learner must never be afraid to be both personal and eclectic with the information. We must decide what the information means to us personally, and, at the same time, be willing to see many other points of view.

The best leaders are usually passionate learners. Being a student of life endears the leader to the follower. Once we decide that our learning is complete, we offer little value to the development of the team. We must share the knowledge and systems of the past in order to develop the thinking of tomorrow.

Teaching and instruction must prepare us for the work ahead. A prepared workforce will give you the bench strength to weather the most significant of challenges. A prepared workforce will trust leadership. Many young workers of today are leaving organizations because they are not prepared to handle the complex people and system challenges they face on the job.

"People change when they hurt enough that they have to, learn enough that they want to, or receive enough that they are able to."
~John Maxwell

CHAPTER 22

The Peter Principle is Real!

The Peter Principle states, "In a hierarchy, employees tend to rise to their level of incompetence."

Dr. Laurence J. Peter and Raymond Hull in their 1968 book, *The Peter Principle*, introduced the "salutary science of Hierarchiology." The principle states that in any hierarchy, members are promoted, so long as they work competently. Eventually, they are promoted to a position at which they are no longer competent, or their "level of incompetence." And there they remain.

Peter's corollary states, "In time, every position tends to be occupied by an employee who is incompetent to carry out the duties." Furthermore, "Work is accomplished by those employees who have not yet reached their level of incompetence." Do you know anyone like this?

To succeed in the coming business climate, successful organizations will avoid the Peter Principle by focusing on employee development. In this way, they will ensure that the most competent people occupy each position within the company.

Companies that fail to develop current organizational talent will face enormous pressure for survival. Though it may seem self-explanatory, creating a competitive advantage is often challenging to say the least. Effective learning experiences that promote application on the job are not easy to develop. The challenge of development and the difficulty to determine the return on investment are the most significant barriers to developing a winning team.

Training and development can be exploited as a competitive advantage if you do not try to hedge your bets or focus on price alone.

Amidst the competitive challenge, most companies opt to do nothing and remain in the herd. Separating the herd is difficult. It is, however, what keeps your business thriving when others are struggling.

Whatever competitive advantage you seek, the medium for successful implementation is the learning organization that can adapt to frequent and demanding changes in the market. Consider what makes you do business with one organization over another. The quality of the product, the taste of the food, the appearance of the facility, and the competency of the people are all by-products of an amazing training and development system. Unless you are the only employee and you are finished learning, you will have to develop others to be successful in the same manner.

Yet, too many organizations exert control as a competitive advantage. Leaders are fooling themselves if they think they control the actions of their employees. Individuals are going to do what they want to do. That might mean complying with a request or not. Employees can also say one thing and do another. Ultimately, they can also opt to leave your organization for "greener pastures." We really only influence each other's actions.

Following are five clues that you may have control issues with your team:

1. Yelling and screaming are common behaviors.

2. Low trust and morale are prevalent.

3. People leave your organization "suddenly" for unusual or unexplained reasons.

4. Results are inconsistent and sporadic among groups.

5. Personalities, rather than values, guide most behavior.

Another shortcut organizations attempt to avoid is proper training. Development is the promotion of the good "operator" (this could also be a salesperson, engineer, welder, painter, artist, or programmer) to a leadership position. The "Super Operator" is possibly a key person on your team, but when they are promoted to supervisor, with little or no training, they struggle. They don't have the tools to be successful. Their leaders assumed they would make a good supervisor because they know the production or business process. Simply put, process and technical knowledge is only one small part of the skills necessary to be a successful leader.

Additionally, many Super Operators dislike the duties of an effective leader. They take the job because it is the only way they can grow financially. They hate the job because they have never been taught how to confront others. They tend to skip activities they are not prepared to do.

Unfortunately, these individuals tend to settle in new leadership roles, and remain there until they retire or decide to leave. Thus, the Peter Principle emerges within the company. They have been promoted to their level of incompetency, and there they will remain until someone takes action.

Example:

A moderately sized business was struggling. The supervisors were selected because of their talent as operators, and they were given little training.

I visited with the manager about the development of these leaders, and his comments caught me a bit off guard. He stated that if he invested the time to develop his supervisors, they might leave his company for greener pastures.

I pondered the significance of his message. Excellence is something people can actually be afraid of. Is this why so many companies avoid training and development?

Admitting there is a need to develop your team truly does expose cracks and faults. Often, incremental employee development is better than pushing too much too fast. People can only absorb so much information at a time. Yet, we have to make information and training available in as concentrated doses as possible.

After all, if our companies are going to be successful, we have to seek excellence at all levels of the organization. In this way, we will avoid falling prey to the Peter Principle.

**"Out of clutter, find simplicity.
From discord, find harmony.
In the middle of difficulty lies opportunity."**
~Albert Einstein

CHAPTER 23

Dysfunction Begets Dysfunction

Too many leaders ignore team problems, hoping that behaviors will improve over time. Unfortunately, problems only gets worse, and everyone suffers. Team dynamics are a direct consequence of action or inaction by leadership.

Organizational wounds may appear to heal, yet they are only masking the problems that remain. Scar tissue builds, and team members become disillusioned that things will "never" get better.

It is at this point that you begin to experience a "talent exodus" that worsens as the quality of your team's performance drops. Your team experiences a shift that collects the "bottom of the barrel." The most talented members begin to search for, and will eventually find, opportunity with another team.

When one person begins causing a problem for the team, and leaders don't take action, the morale of the team diminishes. The situation amplifies as the problem persists. Hope for improvement feels futile as the entire team loses collective productivity. People no longer give that extra effort; why should they when leadership fails to address the problem? So the spiral worsens.

Following are symptoms of dysfunction within teams:

- Communication exists in silos. Politics and coalitions prevent honest and meaningful communication.

- Conflict is common. Missing goal alignment creates effort that opposes other efforts on the team.

- Stress levels are high. Temper and emotional response is very common.

- Trust is missing. People simply do not trust each other, and refuse to work together.

- Blame replaces accountability. People are posturing for individuals, rather than the team.

According to Patrick Lencioni, the five dysfunctions of a team are:

1. Absence of trust
2. Fear of conflict
3. Lack of commitment
4. Avoidance of accountability
5. Inattention to results

These "symptoms" of the leadership disease are perpetuated by incompetence and ignorance. The dysfunctional managers are either incapable of understanding and applying methodology, or they are ignorant of the value created by real leadership.

So, what do you do? There are two potential solutions for team dysfunction. First, team interventions can work if the facilitation is tough and candid. People must feel safe to speak freely without fear of consequences.

The second potential solution is to remove the problem person. This approach cleanses the organization immediately. Often, those remaining wonder what took so long.

In order to trust our leaders, we must be willing to give, and make ourselves vulnerable. Fear and respect are not synonymous, yet too many managers simply do not understand the difference. When we fear for our own safety, our natural instinct becomes self-preservation. Simply put, fear of failure must be minimized in your environment in order to maximize trust. Otherwise, the dysfunction remains and success becomes rare.

There are two types of organizational conflict. Destructive conflict leads to a win-lose, while constructive conflict often leads to win-win.

Destructive conflict promotes a clear winner, and an even clearer loser. No matter how it may be perceived in the short-term, destructive conflict eventually results in both parties losing. The winning party eventually loses the trust and respect of the other party, and begins to have very little influence on the team.

Fearing constructive conflict is more common than most like to admit. The prevalence of so many passive-aggressive personalities is evidence that humans opt to avoid conflict in the attempt to get along with each other.

Learning to differentiate between destructive and constructive conflict takes commitment and practice by an aspiring leader. Skill in this area can be developed through repetition. Many turn to executive coaches who act as a sounding board to develop this skill.

A lack of commitment is another challenge facing too many organizations. These organizations are often riddled with mediocrity due to the Peter Principle, and performance simply is not a prerequisite for continued employment.

The lack of commitment often grows into a sense of entitlement. When this happens, people begin to take their job for granted. Simply showing up becomes normal, and expectations for excellence become a distant memory.

A lack of commitment also exists when an organization has little value in human contribution. When the human talent becomes less valuable to the leadership team, the reciprocal commitment is realized. Ignorant and incompetent managers have created the very lack of commitment they curse today. Never underestimate the critical fact that a comprehensive, organizational lack of commitment is a reflection of the attitude from management.

On the other hand, the company that cares about every employee will galvanize commitment. Placing people first may sound familiar, but it is actually rare.

The thing about a tough economy is that it removes the leadership camouflage that sometimes grows "to excess" when times are good. Similarly, in the tough reality of winter, the leaves and foliage are thinned, so what may have been hidden is now exposed.

Recently, a number of companies have discussed the challenges of creating a more "accountable" culture. Unfortunately, accountability is one of the most abused, and poorly utilized, words in business today. Many dictionaries misdefine this word as a synonym for responsibility. In reality, the words are not even similar. The root word for accountability is "count," while the root word for responsibility is "respond."

We have interchanged these words for so long that we don't blink when they are used in error. The truth is, accountability (the ability to count) is much more complex than a simple definition can encompass.

Some leaders confuse accountability with blame. "Who are you going to hold accountable?" is often "code" for looking for someone to blame.

Other leaders micro-manage as a way to hold subordinates accountable. In reality, they micro-mange for one of two reasons: First, they don't want subordinates to fail, so they "over manage" to protect someone from accountability. Second, leaders simply don't trust that the subordinate will perform the job.

Either way, the subordinate fails to succeed or learn from possible mistakes. As a leader, it is up to you to set a good balance between authority and empowerment to ensure that every person acts with accountability.

We cannot "hold" people accountable until they are given the resources, rules, and protection to be held accountable. The resources to be successful are necessary, whether it be training, equipment, or money. Withholding these resources limits accountability greatly.

The rules of the game are the policies and guidelines for the team. If the team members do not know what they can and cannot do, they cannot be held accountable for performance.

Finally, the team must be allowed to fail in order to succeed. The leader must protect them, and accept failure, in order to get the most effort from each person. If failure is not tolerated—even though it is inevitable—we begin to hedge our bets to protect ourselves. This tendency creates hesitation that limits organizational accountability and performance.

Are honest mistakes allowed on your team? Do people fear failing to the point that they become paralyzed at decision time? Are mistakes treated as opportunities for development? John Maxwell, in his book *Failing Forward*, states that honest mistakes should actually be encouraged, not just tolerated.

Think of it this way, if people on your team are not making mistakes, what are they doing? They probably opt to do nothing rather than taking a chance for success.

What exactly is an honest mistake? If my son spills his milk at the dinner table, I cannot get angry because I too will eventually spill my milk. However, if my son is throwing his football at the dinner table and spills his milk, it is no longer an honest mistake. If someone does something they know they shouldn't, we should focus on the behavior, rather than the end result.

As leaders, we must learn to focus on the behavior first, and the result second. The best leaders use honest mistakes as learning opportunities, and they create a culture of positive risk taking for the team. In this environment, people are not afraid to fail, as long as the attempt is honest and in the benefit of the organization.

This is very difficult in our myopic culture. We live by a flawed corporate culture that mortgages the very future of the organizations we serve. This is driven by an insatiable need for short-term success like stock price and quarterly earnings results.

Results really do matter. Typically, companies define results by trailing indicators of success; they should measure results by leading indicators. In other words, the best leaders understand that you reward the work that leads to results. This emphasis on the long-term, at the expense of the short-term, is the difference between an enduring winner and an occasional winner.

Attention to results is so misunderstood that leaders often have no clue how results are achieved. Most companies do not know if they are profitable until after the measurement period is over.

Imagine playing a game for several hours with no score or method for finding out whether or not you are winning or losing. How would you make adjustments during the game?

How would your team feel? This flaw in how companies play the game often results in apathy and disrespect on the team. If leaders punish the unknowing team members for their lack of achievement, the employees feel abused and exploited because they didn't know how they were being measured, or what the score was during the game.

So, what steps can you take to make sure you have a winning team? Following are some tips to better improve your team for high performance:

1. Schedule regular team building activities, such as retreats and interactive group training.

2. Require team members to work on problems and projects with those they don't routinely interact with at work.

3. Make group assignments randomly to promote further interaction.

4. Hold events that promote bonding, such as meals or other social gatherings.

5. Be aware that teams will tend to split into subgroups based on friendship and comfort.

"Intelligence plus character is the true meaning of education."
~Martin Luther King, Jr.

CHAPTER 24

Is My Boss an Idiot?

We have all had an idiot for a boss at some point in our lives. For some of us, that pain is a present reality, and for others, it is a painful memory. Maybe you will have one in the future.

For younger workers, the problem with idiot bosses is more pronounced. Today's high-technology work force resists being led by traditional, short-term focused managers and supervisors. They not only view these leaders as idiots, they will also ignore directives and quickly seek employment with companies that have better leadership. In the past, idiot bosses could get away with their antics through fear and intimidation, but the current generation will not put up with this treatment.

Today's tough economy removes the natural camouflage that historically concealed the struggling managers. These bosses seem to succeed when the economy was robust and anyone is making money. But business stress makes the bad leaders stand out in the crowd. Every mistake they make has a more critical impact on the performance of the business. When the bad economy places more pressure on the organization, the decisions and corresponding results become amplified.

When leadership is ineffective, the best and most talented members of your team will leave the company. Meanwhile, the average and under-performing employees will stay because they know their options are limited in a competitive job market. If you conduct exhaustive and detailed exit interviews of those choosing to leave your company, you will discover that management and supervision are probably the cause, especially among your younger and more talented workers.

At this point, you should check to see if communication among your team is limited to problems and challenges, while the positive success of your team goes ignored. The younger generation thrives on information. Managers and supervisors cannot share too much business information with today's young worker. The need to process information (good and bad) is critical to keep workers engaged on the job. Positive feedback is not only necessary; it is mandatory to keep the best workers engaged.

Part of that desire for information involves training and development resources. The informed younger worker understands that in tough economic times, they are going to be asked to do more with less. Intuitively, they have a clear understanding that learning becomes a competitive necessity, rather than optional luxury.

Alternatively, younger workers seek social acceptance at work. Successful organizations of the future will make "fun at work" an imperative. If a young worker cannot experience some form of social connection at work, their priority will be on finding an organization that will provide a connection. The idea that "we are here to work" is simply not embraced by the emerging workforce of today.

Historically, most managers did not understand that morale equals productivity. Management did not consider good morale as a prerequisite for the optimization of productivity. For some organizations, morale was even viewed as irrelevant. These organizations often managed by fear and intimidation. Some used overt methods to create fear, while in other organizations the fear was more subtle.

When times are tough, some managers make it more difficult for team members to perform daily functions. The need to control spending and waste can actually become more costly to the organization. Today's young worker understands that resources are important. However, they also understand that the amount of time it takes to get a resource can be more critical than the actual cost of the resource. This critical understanding of time value has been developed by the very technology that made them who they are today. Search engines and smart phones have created an impatient workforce that demands solutions immediately. Struggling managers often cannot comprehend the inherent need in a young worker to make the most valuable use of their time, while performing the work that they have been assigned.

Today's work environment must adapt quickly to survive the pending generational storm. Most managers acknowledge that change is occurring, yet they are doing very little to prepare for the future that change will bring.

On paper, and in most polite conversations, these same managers agree that the quality of a business team or organization is based on the quality of the employees. Yet, they contradict themselves every day. Many managers have actually become more cynical about the value of the human element in businesses. Too many organizations are ignoring the canyon between the supervisor of past, and the young worker of the present.

The concept of servant leadership is fading quickly. Most organizations simply do not consider people and talent as the competitive advantage. They make the worker less valuable than the machines or other property in the organization. This is a subtle and gradual process that is magnified greatly by the natural peaks and valleys of business.

Imagine a business serving a market that moves up and down every two to three years. Now imagine the employment level in this business. It may add or lose up to 70% of its employees each time the market falls and recovers. It is only natural, over a 20 to 30 year period for the managers to become callused to the value of the individual contributor.

These same managers may even choose to limit their human connection in order to make the next round of layoffs easier on themselves. They will naturally resist forming attachments to the people they know will be gone with the next swing of the market.

This loss of human value in the workplace, combined with the emergence of today's young worker, is significant. If we are not careful, we can lose value in what is most precious in today's organization—our people. This loss of human value will certainly not be intentional for most organizations. They will simply become "battle scarred" during tough economic times, and begin to rationalize the incomprehensible.

World-class companies know that the best people are needed to help them weather any economic storm. Great leaders will re-clarify and re-amplify the value of the best people on the team. They will certainly not take this talent for granted, or remove them to save a dollar.

The idiot bosses, on the other hand, will find no value in the people that make them successful. They will only see the financial statements, without regard for the humans behind the numbers. The results of this attitude will cripple their company, and limit their potential for success in the coming economy.

The young worker of today has been placed on a proverbial pedestal by their parents. From this position, they will not allow themselves to be retained by an organization that does not recognize their value. Nor will they be attracted to companies with ineffective leadership. They will simply reciprocate the same sense of value to the organization.

The younger workforce wants to be part of something meaningful, where they can make a difference. They want to create and maintain critical social connections at work. They want to have fun while doing meaningful work. Above all, they want to be fed constantly with information that they can process, while performing whatever activities they are being paid to perform.

Any environment that does not give them what they need will be shunned. Their contribution will always be limited to the investment that companies make in them. And they will eventually seek what they desire elsewhere.

"The waiting is the hardest part."
~Tom Petty

CHAPTER 25

Does Being Nice Make a Difference?

Can being nice impact the bottom line? Do we sometimes neglect the very people that mean success or failure in the game of business? Does being mean, rude, or hostile with employees increase production?

Remember that the secret mission of my book, *Leadership Among Idiots*, is to eradicate, or at least control, the epidemic of "idiocy" that infects so many bosses. Many of these bosses actually believe that being nice to employees will get less effort from them. They believe that being nice is a sign of weakness.

What a tragic view of the human condition. I believe we can be pleasant and firm at the same time. We can be nice to our employees, and still give them the consistency and fairness they prefer. Positive reinforcement does increase positive behavior. It is not a contradiction to be nice to your employees, and still maintain trust and respect.

Second, think of being nice in the application of sales. The first, and often most neglected, rule of sales states that people want to do business with people they like. In other words, we will often pay MORE to do business with people that we enjoy being around. In contrast, we will take our business elsewhere quickly if we don't feel a connection to a sales person or business. Yet, we have all experienced bad customer service to the point that we really notice good customer service when we see it.

Oddly enough, exceptional customer service now seems to be the exception, rather than the norm. It simply blows my mind! Companies will spend millions of dollars to get a customer to walk in the door, and spend little to nothing teaching employees how to treat customers once they are there!

Finally, think about the millions of bosses who don't value the very people that make them successful. Think about the many employees who are willing to leave their current job as soon as something better comes along.

Even more remarkable are the statements that I hear when confronting the leaders. They say things like, "They get a paycheck, don't they?" or "I don't have time for being nice."

Tragically, many will find out too late how important job satisfaction is to the new workforce. Only when their talent starts leaving will they realize the tremendous cost of losing a good employee.

I predict that we will see 'a very large "spike" in turnover cost for businesses as the economy recovers, Baby Boomers retire, and young talent becomes difficult to acquire. The "musical chairs" is about to begin, and some companies are going to end up with the "left-over employees," those that others do not want.

How can we be nice, and avoid the consequences of negative attitudes toward employees? Following are a few steps to get started:

1. Recognize that you have neglected to clarify, role-model, and reinforce the values for your team. Decision making is easy when values are clear!

2. Make it a daily mission to let your team know the "main thing" for your organization: customer service, safety, quality, etc.

3. DO NOT assume your leaders know how to be leaders. Provide them with the tools to be successful.

4. Lead by example. Be nice and watch your bottom line grow. I love the quote from Abraham Lincoln, "Do not confuse my kindness as weakness."

What gets in the way of niceness? What causes break downs and conflicts? Faulty communication. We tend to assume our communication is effective, but can you name a major issue in your company that was not rooted in poor communication or a lack of communication?

As stress impacts our businesses, conflict tends to become more prevalent. Many individuals simply don't know how to handle difficult people or conflict. They tend to be better at talking *about* people, rather than *to* people.

How do you know your team is experiencing conflict? Following are five symptoms:

1. Communication exists in silos. People build coalitions that prevent honest and meaningful communication.

2. There is a lack of goal alignment. People work against each other, instead of with each other.

3. Stress levels are high. People walk around "on edge" with a hair-trigger temper.

4. Trust is absent. People do not work to build and maintain trust.

5. Team members don't understand the differ-
    ence between accountability and blame.

In the winning organization, accountability and forgiveness are complimentary to each other. But what happened to forgiveness in business? Accountability and forgiveness are not mutually exclusive concepts.

The strange thing about forgiveness is how selective we are with who gets it. Why do we forgive some, and not others? Why are some people forever on our hit list, while others seem to be forgiven quickly? We tend to forgive (or not) based on the relationship we have with the person in question.

In business, we may not "have to" forgive in order to maintain the working relationship. We may "hold on" to the negative feelings toward a co-worker for years. I have seen cases with two individuals disliking each other for years when the original reason may have been long forgotten. Oddly enough, they dislike each other, but cannot remember exactly why they feel the way they do. To forgive, or not to forgive, is based on the relation-ship between the people involved.

Think of it this way, if there is equity in our "rela-tionship bank account," we are more willing to for-give. If the account is empty (or worse, overdrawn) we are far less likely to forgive the other person. With our spouses and children, we make deposits on a recurring basis through normal activities together.

We make deposits with our friends through interaction and conversation. But we do not have the same mechanism in the workplace. Often, we have to go the extra mile to make sure we are investing in the relationship bank accounts at work.

We usually are not required to interact on a personal level on the job. Many "relationship bank accounts" go unattended, and are ultimately ignored. A mother will forgive a murdering child, while a coworker is "written off" forever for a comment made many years ago.

The best way to encourage investments in relationship bank accounts in the workplace is to bring employees together, have them interact with each other in more social environments, such as retreats or team-building activities. You might also want to assign tasks randomly to bring different people together at different times. There are many things.

Above all, we as leaders must lead by example. Make sure that you not only forgive your employees and co-workers, but that they know they have been forgiven.

"A pessimist sees the difficulty in every opportunity;
an optimist sees the opportunity in every difficulty."
~Winston Churchill

CHAPTER 26

Is Mediocrity Contagious?

What is happening to our next generation of leaders? Have we become a nation that inspires mediocrity? Are we going through a metamorphosis, and don't realize it? Do we really believe excellence comes without effort? Are we all getting infected with the mediocrity disease?

When I think of mediocrity, and how it is created and perpetuated, what comes to mind is how we give out "participation" trophies for anyone who shows up to a sporting event. In an effort to make all the players happy, everyone gets a trophy. Is happiness what we truly seek? Have we lost the intestinal fortitude to inspire hard work and better effort for the reward? Should everyone pass, and none fail? Do we really appreciate anything that comes too easy?

Maybe this phenomenon is rooted in a generation of Americans that has an entitled view of the world—they are owed something because of their very existence. Maybe our own need to make things better for our children has caused them to expect so much as young adults.

As a parent of two boys, I am often guilty of giving too much to my children. Yet, as a society, we have become infected by the same need to give a hand-out, instead of a hand-up.

True personal value comes from the sense of accomplishment. Think about something you worked hard to achieve. The struggle probably made the accomplishment more valuable to you. You wouldn't be as proud of that accomplishment if it came easily.

Supply-and-demand economics describes this situation. What is plentiful and easy to acquire has little value, while that which is obtained through difficulty, or is rare, holds precious value. You will not respect, nor hold as valuable, that which is easily obtained and plentiful.

True reward comes from the struggle to improve. Whether it is sports, education, or owning a home, there is great value in the struggle to achieve. Determination, and stubbornness to work hard for the end-result, is what I hope to inspire in my two boys. Similarly, achievement without effort is useless for us as individuals and as organizations.

Great leaders understand that effort yields greatness. Only true meritocracy can inspire world-class results. On the other hand, entitlement can be the virus that kills the host. If the workforce falls into mediocrity, the whole organization will suffer and eventually fail.

In today's self-focused work environment, employees are drawn to leaders who inspire for a larger purpose. I believe our employees have a "sixth sense" that can easily discern whether we are working for ourselves or for others. Those who are truly selfless will be magnetic to a new generation of followers.

A recent *USA Today* survey stated that only 48% of "bosses" were likeable. Imagine if the question were asked a bit differently. What percentage of bosses truly inspire us to be better performers? I imagine a much smaller number.

Think about the cost this has on your organization. What does unrealized performance cost your company or organization in a year? There is hope, and I have seen leaders who truly inspire our new generation in the workplace.

The new generation of workers can truly be inspired! Generation Y is more willing to volunteer for a cause than other generations. Where does this giving come from? The answer is simple, yet profound. We have given to these workers so much that they have come to expect so much. With perceived abundance, the need to stay in a job was minimal. After all, they could always get another job.

Studying and researching recent employment trends has revealed an amazing truth about current organizational dynamics. Our new generation of workers magnifies a reality that exists in all of us. We really do want to be inspired to be better—better parents, spouses, and performers at work. We want to belong, compete, and succeed.

Understanding this, you should give your team a sense of a belonging as you work toward a meritocracy, thus promoting success at all levels of your organization. When this happens, your team will outperform past successes, and you will find an illusive, hidden capacity in your team.

Leaders seeking only their self-interest cannot see this simple truth! Their pursuits are plagued by a vision of self and self-purpose that makes them literally blind to the vision of service to others. They are not necessarily bad people. They are merely handicapped with an inability to see beyond themselves.

True leaders, on the other hand, have the vision of selflessness that draws followers like a moth to a light. The word *leadership* logically implies followship. Someone must decide to follow the leader for some reason.

Why do we follow another person? When you boil down the complexities of human behavior, the primary reasons we follow someone else are very basic. First, we see a personal benefit in following the person. We see the methodology they utilize as better than our current method, or we perceive that following them will make it easier to accomplish a given task or goal.

Second, the leader actually influences our thinking. They inspire us to obtain more than we have. This cognitive influence is the more complex of the two pillars of leadership. Following the lead of others is as basic as human nature. We replicate behavior that produces desired results. Humans have always followed the leader.

The cumulative and iterative nature of learning produces leadership that builds upon the success and failure of the past. Technology and invention are great examples of the human need to improve a better way to exist.

Influencing the thinking of another human to see a different point of view is difficult. Our cognitive awareness is the product of both genetics and environment. To a smaller degree, our personality will influence our thinking. For instance, someone who is shy and inhibited will not desire nor readily develop a point of view that includes behavior that might be interpreted as extroverted. These individuals may find more value in behavior that is less obvious to others. On the other hand, an individual with an outgoing personality may lead others with similar tendencies and replicate similar behavior.

Our environment plays a significant role in our ever-changing mental picture. Our experiences, and the information we gather, are constantly changing the portal by which we view the world. The changing viewpoint can be very subtle or very significant, depending on the severity of the experience or the influence of the leader. In other words, we all experience those life altering events that leave an indelible mark on our view of the world.

Influencing the thinking of another human can be both passive and active. We can be totally aloof, and others will follow our lead if they see our point of view as interesting or beneficial. Such leaders are followed because of other basic human tendencies, such as admiration or envy. We admire another individual, and attempt to follow the logic of their thinking.

While not always accurate, this perception becomes our reality. This is often manifested by an unsuccessful attempt to copy or mimic a philosophy. Without the background or experience of the individual, it becomes difficult, if not impossible, to truly replicate a philosophy.

The intentional influence of another human is a bit more challenging because the other individual may not desire, nor see the benefit of, the change.

This leadership requires patience and deliberate effort.

Influential leadership only takes place once the other person decides our point of view is personally beneficial to them. They then make a conscious decision to adopt the new thinking as their own.

In other words, as parents we slowly influence the thinking of our children in both a positive and negative manner. We can prescribe a point of view that is beneficial, as well as harmful, through our actions as parents.

Amazingly, the leader who applies deliberate effort to influence others positively can make improvements in the leadership they exert on both the people and the organization they serve. Taking the time to be aware of our influence, through our actions and our words, is a skill that can be both taught and learned. Being positive with others, looking for ways to help others succeed, and being humble about success are all methods to influence others. People want to follow those who make them feel good, or that make their lives better.

A supervisor who develops the talent and capability of others will be seen as a giving person that others are drawn to in business. A manager who looks for the positive in situations that present the most challenge, will be attractive to followers. An executive who creates a significant purpose for the organization will be the inspiration to others. Mark

Zuckerberg's desire to create something "cool" with Facebook made it a household name that might very well change the course of humanity. Similarly, Steve Jobs' creativity and ability have made Apple the market leader in technology.

Just remember that leadership is indeed a journey, rather than a destination. We are all continually refining and developing the influence we have on others. This influence can be both positive and negative for the follower. After all, some of the most influential leaders in history did not have a positive impact on humanity. Leadership, and the success it may have, will always rest on the desire of the follower. Only the follower gives us the title of leader. And what they give, they can also take away.

Is Mediocrity Contagious

"A smooth sea never made a skillful mariner."
~English Proverb

CHAPTER 27
The Workplace 2020

I cannot believe that I am actually going to write about the year 2020. It almost sounds like a science fiction movie title, and yet, it is only a few short years away. I say "short" because the past decade flew by at an inconceivable pace.

The workplace is changing so fast, and we cannot see (or in some cases deal with) the rate of change we are experiencing. Most companies are stuck in the models of the past, and they are not preparing for the enormity of the future. Imagine the upcoming demand for quality workers, and the pressure companies will have finding talent. In ten years, companies will have more difficulty finding employees than customers.

The workplace in 2020 will be very different from what we see today. Research indicates a major shift that is both intrinsic and extrinsic to most companies. In other words, change will be driven both by the employee and the employment market. Human resources will become more similar to the talent scouts we see in professional sports. Proven talent will cost a premium, while the promise of talent will be held in suspicion. Your resume and credentials alone will not get you in the door.

Highly educated and skilled workers will be represented by "agents" that will sell their capability to the highest bidder. Employment packages will be pre-negotiated, and contracts will lean heavily in the favor of the worker. These proven employees will be in control, and the companies that seek their talent will either pay for, or settle for, the next level down, depending upon budget and other tangible limitations. Employees will be available; however, the best employees will be difficult to acquire.

The workplace in 2020 will also become an incubator for talent. In an environment where top performers are rare, companies will attempt to "grow their own," so to speak. Emphasis on learning and information will be the competitive advantage for the best organizations. Corporate universities and educational partnerships will be a huge part of the annual budget. Executives will understand that the collection of talent, and its capabilities, will define the winning organization.

Baby Boomers, with their knowledge and experience, will be a distant memory in 2020. The workplace will be dominated by the Generation Y, sprinkled with the small group representing Generation X. And a paradigm shift will have occurred for work and work schedules.

The beginning of the end of the 40-hour work week has already appeared. The old-fashioned preoccupation with time as a measure of work has lost favor, and given way to flexible schedules that pay for output, rather than "sitput" (the tendency of organizations to pay employees to sit or stand for time rather than be productive). Single parents are the norm, and work has been adjusted to accommodate the needs of the newer and smaller family unit. Many people are in jobs that allow a cross-pollination of work-home office concepts, while others simply work around the demands of life, traffic, and other issues.

Loyalty to work will be long gone in 2020. Companies will not expect 20 years of service. Talented contributors will be constantly moving from one opportunity to the next. Employment models and contracts will be based on an 18 to 24 month duration that can be renewed by the agreement of both parties.

The workplace itself will be designed like high end department stores and casinos to get employees in, and keep them them there as long as possible. Resources that make life easier for the employee will become common. Day care and medical services may even be expected in order to attract the best from the talent pool. Workout facilities and nap pods (don't laugh) will be available to keep the workforce energized and refreshed. Restaurants and cafeteria services in the workplace will be the norm, rather than the exception.

Of course, older models of work will still remain in 2020. However, they will become the repository of workers with minimal amounts of talent and flexibility. Struggling organizations that are not financially capable of providing the high-demand workplace will settle for those employees who cannot attain jobs elsewhere. These companies will live, for a time, with poor workers and a lack of individual capability. They may even survive by exploiting immigrant workers. However, the cream of this crop will soon pursue opportunities in progressive organizations.

According to Gallup, you must ask yourself the 12 questions below to learn how your employees measure your workplace:

1. Do I know what is expected of me?

2. Do I have the materials and equipment I need to do my work right?

3. Do I have the opportunity to do what I do best?

4. In the past seven days, have I received recognition or praise?

5. Does anybody at my workplace seem to care about me as a person?

6. Is there anyone who encourages my development?

7. Do my opinions count?

8. Does the mission/purpose of my company make me feel that my job is important?

9. Do I have a best friend at the organization?

10. Has someone talked to me about my progress in the last six months?

11. This last year, has my job given me an opportunity to learn and grow?

12. Are my coworkers committed to accomplishing excellence while performing their job responsibilities?

Example:

Trent is a 27 year old robotic technician in the year 2021. He has a girlfriend, but no other significant ties to his community. He makes a comfortable salary, but is always looking for something to improve his financial and personal position. He has no immediate family where he lives, and he welcomes any opportunity to get back to Eastern Oklahoma where he grew up.

Trent placed his electronic resume on the most popular websites relevant to his specialty. His five years of experience with the same company since college is unusual, and he would not mind considering some change for the future. After all, most of his peers have not been with a company for more than two years. His collegiate friends often tease him about his lack of mobility.

Trent gets an electronic notification on his phone regarding a position with a company in Tulsa, Oklahoma. He believes it is close enough to his home town to allow him to live in his parents home. This might just be the change of scenery Trent is looking for. Things have become stale at work; he does not feel like he is learning or being stretched to perform. In short, he is bored with his current company.

The contract offered by the agent in Tulsa requires an 18 month commitment, and the new company will pay him $144,000.00 over the 18-month period, or $8,000.00 per month before taxes. His productive output only requires that he produce six to eight units per week. The schedule for work is very flexible, and, as long as the units are completed by the Saturday of the preceding week, his hours of work are totally optional. He can work any time, day or night, as long as he is in compliance with the specifications of the contract.

The campus has almost everything a modern workplace should have to attract and keep the best young workers in the country. There are five full-service restaurants offering as much food as employees desire at no cost, and they are open 24 hours a day, 7 days a week. There is a workout facility, complete with a gymnasium and indoor swimming complex. The company has a medical clinic and full-time physician. Additionally, the campus offers housing for employees at a minimal cost to encourage the option of no daily commute.

Even more attractive to Trent are the six universities with satellite campuses for him to quench his never ending thirst for knowledge and information.

Trent struggles with the choice of taking this job, or waiting for the next offer. He receives about three similar notifications each week, but this company sits where he is interested in relocating. The money is somewhat less than other offers, but the location could be the deciding factor; after all, he can always accept a more lucrative offer in a couple years. With that realization, Trent accepts the contract.

EPILOGUE
Seek the Anti-ordinary

Closing a book is the most challenging part of writing for me. It is almost like saying goodbye, and I have never been a fan of goodbye.

As you ponder the contents of this book, and the implications of the next ten years, I hope you choose to see this work as a challenge. I hope you take the challenge to grab life by the horns, and make it the very best it can be for you as a leader.

The pending changes we are facing are real, and the speculation contained in this book is going to help those who seek to learn. Too many people will simply react to changes, rather than prepare to make the most of the inevitable. Almost all of the companies I interviewed to complete this book have no formal talent strategy in place, and the rate of talent attrition is accelerating at warp speed, so to speak. Too many leaders are so preoccupied with the present that they cannot see the storm that is upon us.

For those of you who choose to meet the challenge, the next few years are going to be a wonderful opportunity to exercise the leadership skills you have already developed. You are going to see the same reality from a different perspective than most managers. You will be prepared to lead our next generation of talent. You will understand the uniqueness of tomorrow's worker. And, you will be ready to attract what seems to be non-existent in the mass chaos of the new workforce.

Your organization will stand among the ruins of those that did not see the storm coming. Your team will attract the best and brightest, while others will be left to rebuild after the storm is upon us. Your ability to react will seem lucky to those who did not have a plan.

As is the case for those that are usually prepared, your coming success and adaptability will look easy. Others will not see your hard work and deliberate effort to become the employer of preference. They won't understand how you are able to download seemingly endless volumes of knowledge and information from your experienced team before they retire. Or how you are able to transition

that knowledge and information to the new generation of workers through training and team building
exercises.

My desire for your success is more than a valida-
tion of this writing. It is an affirmation for all the
hard work and determination you have endured to
be successful. While many sports analogies seem to
fit this sentiment, success on the field is usually preceded by many hours of dedicated hard work that
no one else sees, or, in some cases, understands.
Excellence is a choice we make deliberately.

While the word *extraordinary* is common, I do
not think it adequately fits my challenge for you.
The ordinary company is going to become a victim
of the future. I want each reader, and the organization they represent, to become "anti-ordinary."
Anti-ordinary is a deliberate effort to be other than
ordinary. It is the manifestation of an individual or
organization's desire to be anything but ordinary.
Extraordinary is ordinary but better. Anti-ordinary
is other than ordinary. After all, your effort and hard
work have made you much more than ordinary.

Ordinary organizations will continue to do
ordinary things, much like ordinary people. The
ant-ordinary organizations will be in the ideal
position to attract and maintain the anti-ordinary
employee. The mass retirement of Baby-Boomer
talent, combined with the integration of Generation
Y into the mainstream labor market, will be a great

opportunity for the prepared, anti-ordinary organizations of the future.

I believe that some people and organizations actually fear excellence, and opt to remain ordinary. The anonymity of being ordinary can be a safe place to exist when the pressure of excellence is so great. Often, the reality of being ordinary can be more comfortable than the scrutiny that comes with higher expectations. Some may even choose failure when something new or different is required, or in the face of an uncertain future.

The pursuit of excellence, or the anti-ordinary, can be very lonely and isolating. The masses of the ordinary will not choose to make the same journey toward excellence. Our social needs place great pressure on individuals and organizations to conform to the known, rather than seek the unknown.

This subtle truth about human nature starts as children, accelerates through adolescence, and remains constant as adults. Assimilation is comfortable, and often expected among our peer groups. The one who is different is labeled as odd or out of touch with reality.

From an organizational standpoint, most companies fear taking the first step or leading the market when it is much safer to stand back, and watch the success or failure of successful companies. We rationalize this decision as following the trail, rather than blazing it. Yet, we hold in high esteem, and even envy, the success of those that choose to be different.

The pain and discomfort of change are usually well rewarded. The gain of success seems more attainable from the view of a spectator that is literally ignorant of the hard work that was a prerequisite. The common person will rarely taste the sweet nectar of success that is available only to the anti-ordinary among us. The willingness to invest greatly in anything is always accompanied by the pain and risk of great failure. Yet, there are those few who are willing to endure this pain and sacrifice to achieve what most will never know.

I wish for you the opportunity to taste this nectar in whatever portion of your life you choose. Whether it is personal or professional, we can all seek to be the anti-ordinary in our pursuits.

We are entering a period of acceptance, rather than excellence. If this book inspires you to resist the powerful, and almost irresistible, temptation to accept even one form of mediocrity in your life, I have accomplished my goal!

THE TALENT EXODUS: *John Grubbs*

ABOUT JOHN GRUBBS

John Grubbs, MBA, CSTM, RPIH is the principal consultant and owner of GCI, a high impact training and consulting firm in Texas. He has worked with many well-known companies internationally, in such fields as healthcare, transportation, manufacturing, education, and service organizations.

John has over 16 years of leadership experience, and he is the author of several books, including the popular, Leadership Among Idiots.

John holds degrees in Occupational Safety and Health, Industrial Technology, and a Master of Business Administration with a focus on organizational leadership. He is an affiliate member of the Worldwide Association of Business Coaches, a Registered Professional Industrial Hygienist, and a Certified Senior Technology Manager. John is a current member of the American Society of Safety Engineers, American Industrial Hygiene Association, National Association of Industrial Technology and the American College of Healthcare Executives.

John lives in East Texas with his wife and two sons. When he isn't speaking or writing, John enjoys coaching youth baseball and other family activities.